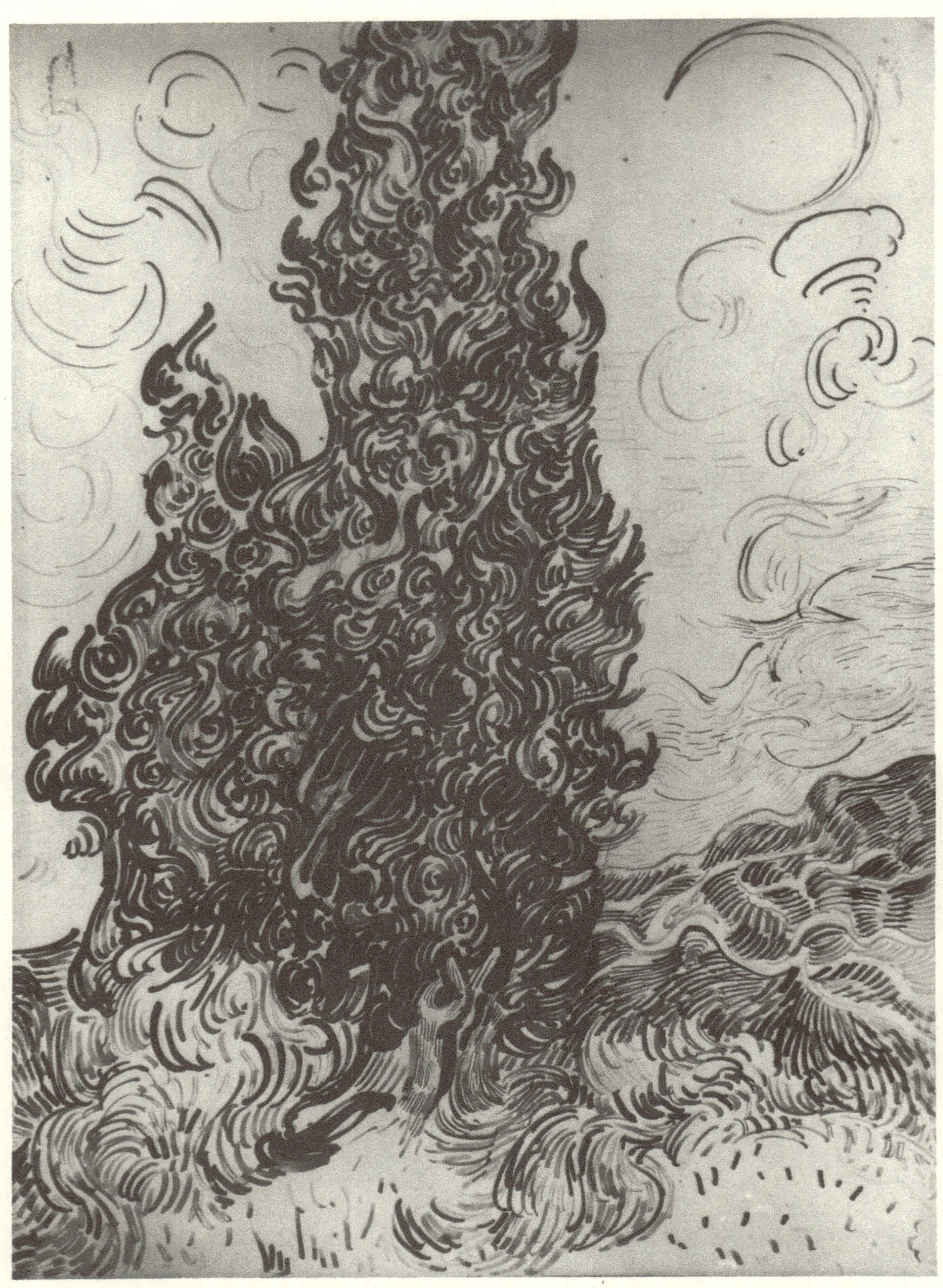

Study for *The Cypresses*. 1889. Reed pen and bistre-colored ink over preparatory pencil; 62.3 × 46.8 cm. (The Brooklyn Museum, 38.123; Frank L. Babbott and A. Augustus Healy Funds.)

VAN GOGH
DRAWINGS

44 Plates by

VINCENT VAN GOGH

Dover Publications, Inc., New York

PUBLISHER'S NOTE

The brief life of Vincent van Gogh, having been the subject of both a popular novel and a motion picture, is perhaps more familiar to the general public than that of any other artist. What follows is a short outline.

Van Gogh was born in The Netherlands in 1853. He worked for the art dealer Goupil & Co., first in The Hague (1869), then in London (1876). By 1880, having unsuccessfully attempted a career as an evangelist, he turned to art. Thus his entire oeuvre is encompassed by the span of a single decade. He received formal training from Anton Mauve and also broadened his knowledge of painting by careful study of the masters. It was Mauve who introduced van Gogh to the works of Millet, which exerted an influence throughout Vincent's career (p. 27). Van Gogh also traveled through The Netherlands, taking as his principal themes peasants, workers and the landscape (pp. 2–11).

In 1888 van Gogh went to Paris to stay with his brother Theo (upon whom he was heavily dependent). He studied briefly in the studio of Fernand Cormon and, more important, met Toulouse-Lautrec, Paul Gauguin, Camille Pissarro and Georges Seurat, and became familiar with Japanese prints. Van Gogh left Paris early in 1888 to work in Arles, a period of unparalleled productivity and artistic development (pp. 15–20, 22–27, 29–35). He persuaded Gauguin to join him, in October, in the "little yellow house" (pp. 32 and 33), but the two did not get on well together and their association ended when van Gogh cut off part of his left ear.

Never all that stable, van Gogh's mental condition deteriorated and in 1889 he committed himself to the asylum at Saint-Rémy-de-Provence (p. 39), where he continued to develop his art, although prone to "attacks." In 1890 he moved to Auvers-sur-Oise, where he committed suicide on July 29.

It is for his paintings, most of them marked by a vivid sense of color and energetic brushwork, that van Gogh is best known. His drawings (done as studies preparatory to paintings, as studies of paintings already executed and as unique works in their own right) reveal the same qualities: With a distinctive rhythmic line, marked by long sensuous strokes punctuated by abrupt strokes and dots, he created color and luminosity in black-and-white works.

The captions, which draw heavily upon information provided by Jan Hulsker in *The Complete Van Gogh*, list subject, date, medium, dimensions (in centimeters, height before width) and the institutions in which they are located.

Van Gogh Drawings: 44 Plates is a new work, first published by Dover Publications, Inc., in 1987.

Library of Congress Cataloging-in-Publication Data

Gogh, Vincent van, 1853–1890.
Van Gogh drawings.

1. Gogh, Vincent van, 1853–1890—Catalogs. 2. Drawing, Dutch—Catalogs. 3. Drawing—19th century—Netherlands—Catalogs. I. Dover Publications, Inc. II. Title.
NC263.G56A4 1987 741.9492 87-16179
ISBN-13: 978-0-486-25485-2
ISBN-10: 0-486-25485-2

Printed in Canada
25485212 2025
www.doverpublications.com

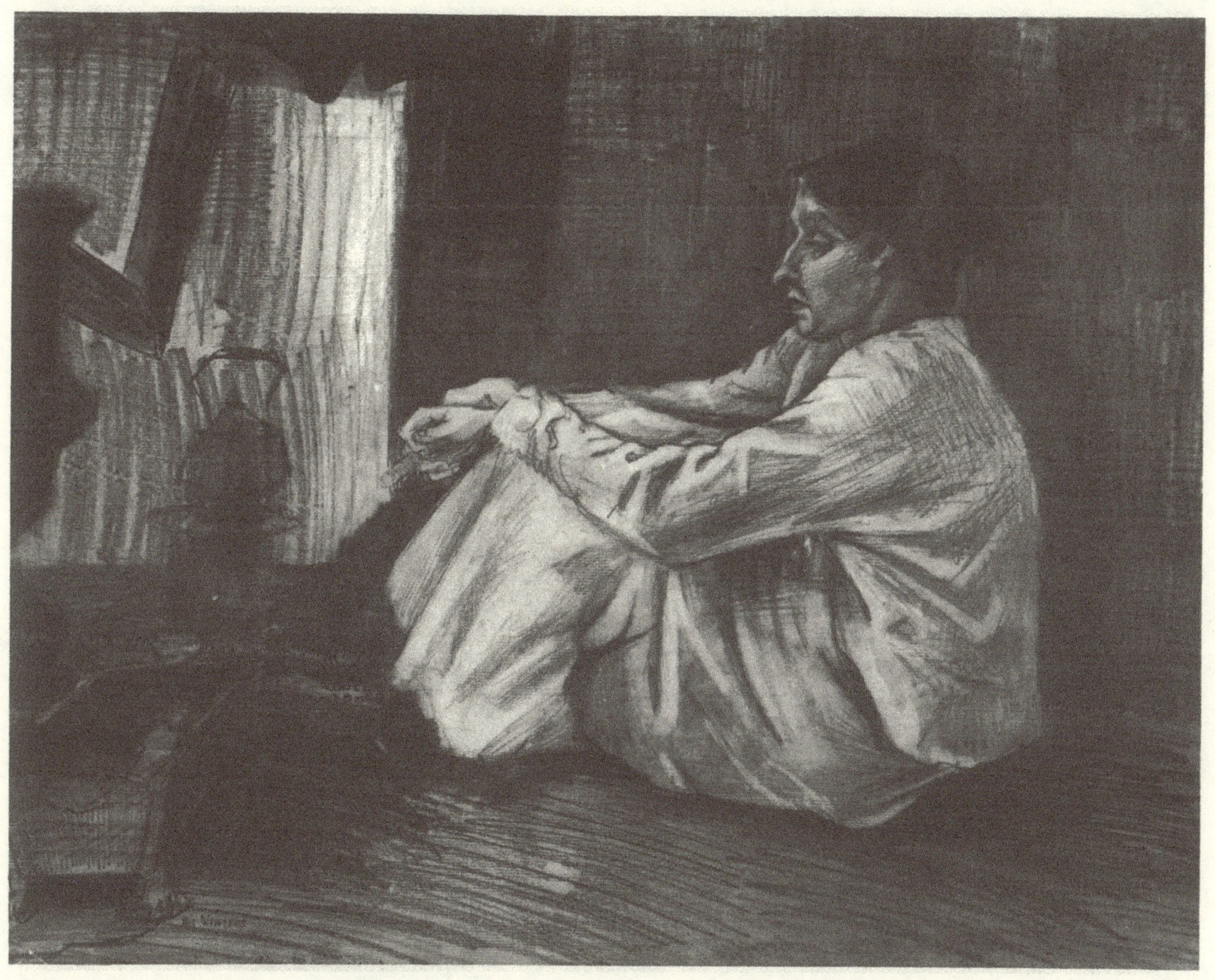

Sien Hoornik with cigar, in white clothes, sitting on the floor by the stove. 1882. Pencil, black chalk, pen, brush and sepia, heightened with white; 45.5 × 56 cm. (State Museum Kröller-Müller, Otterlo, The Netherlands.)

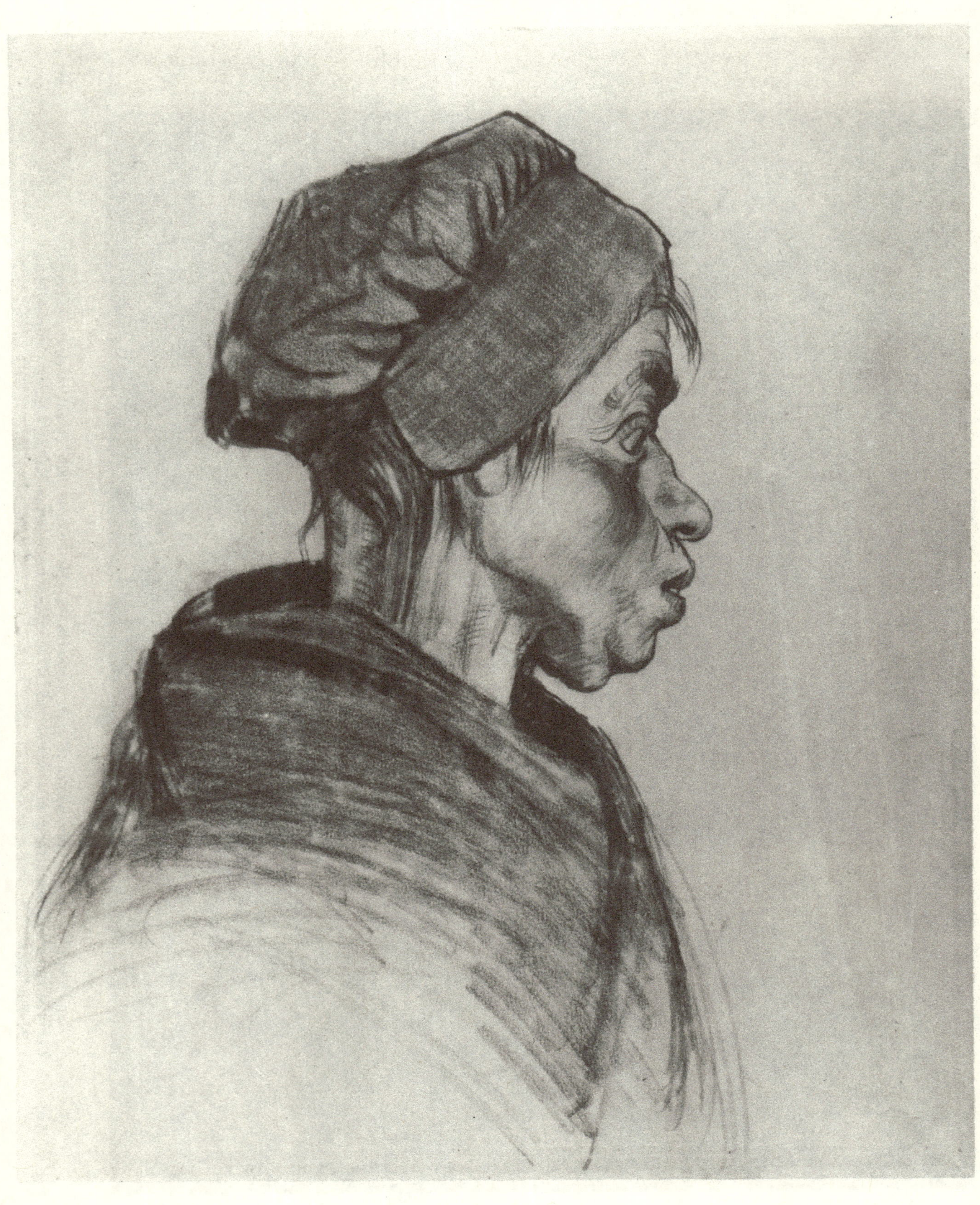

Peasant woman. 1885. Black chalk; 40 × 33 cm. (Van Gogh Foundation/National Museum Vincent van Gogh, Amsterdam.)

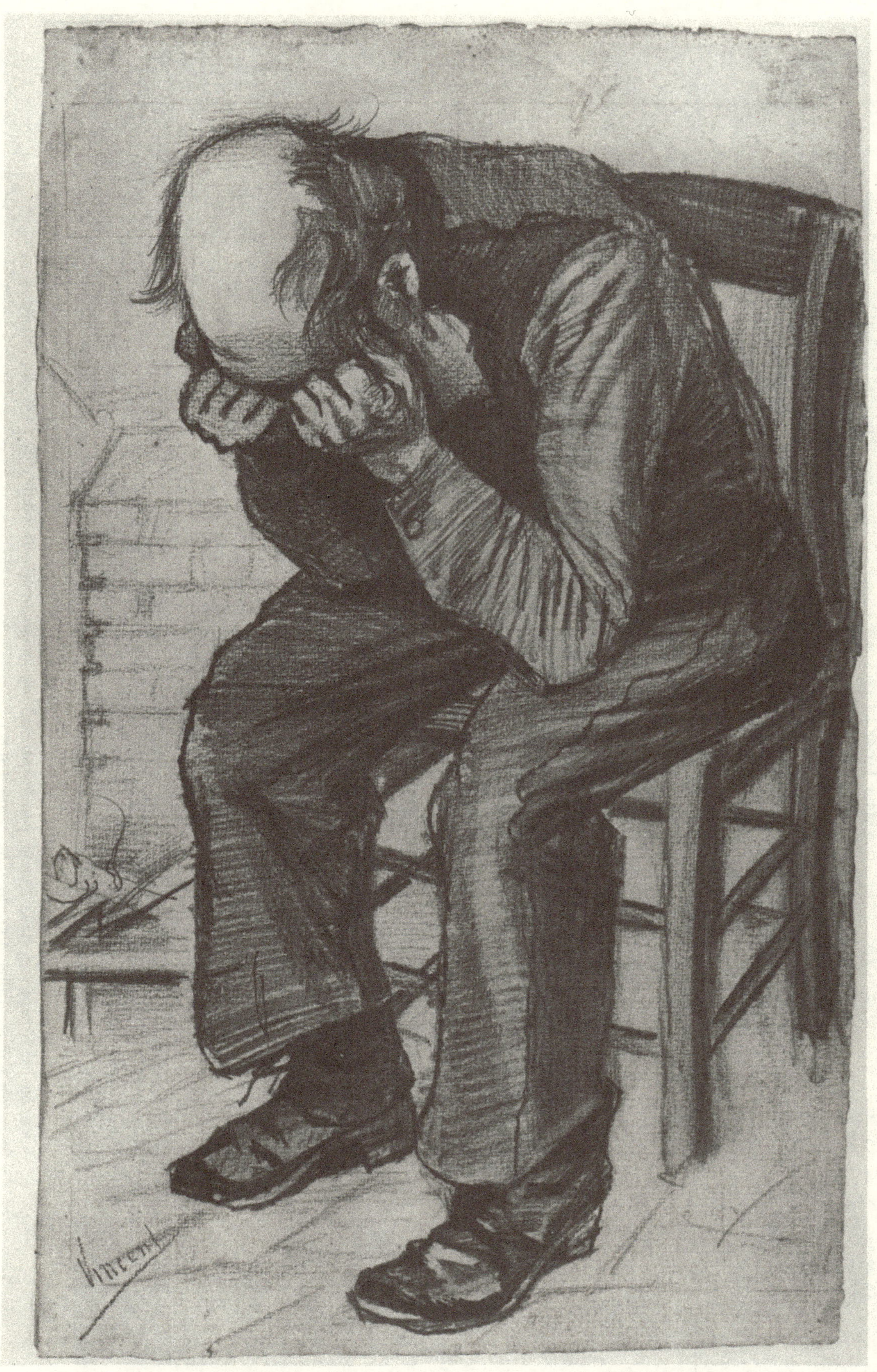

Old man mourning. 1882. Pencil; 50 × 31 cm. (Van Gogh Foundation/National Museum Vincent van Gogh, Amsterdam.)

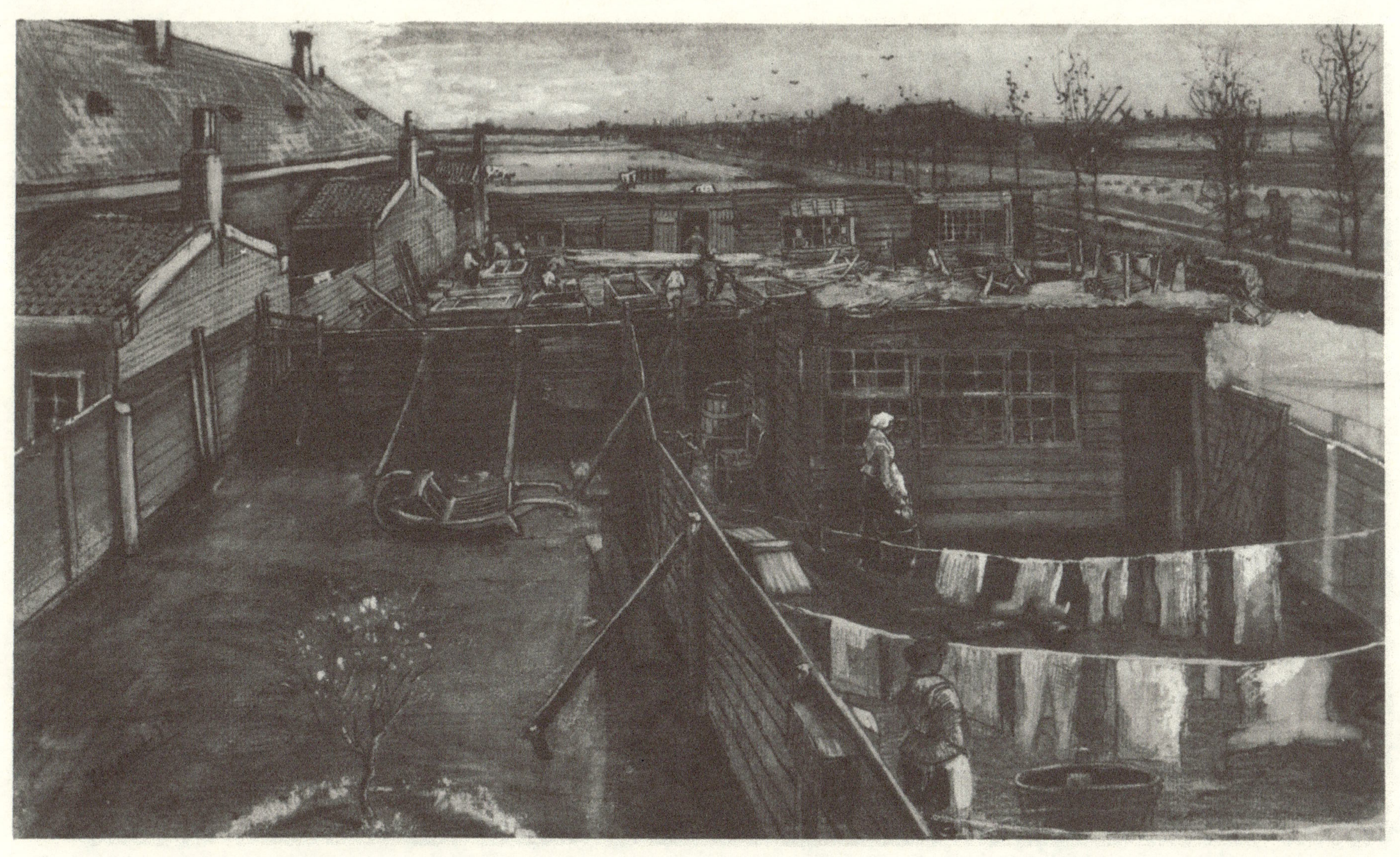

View on the Schenkweg. 1882. Pencil, pen, brush and ink, heightened with white; 28 × 47 cm. (State Museum Kröller-Müller, Otterlo, The Netherlands.)

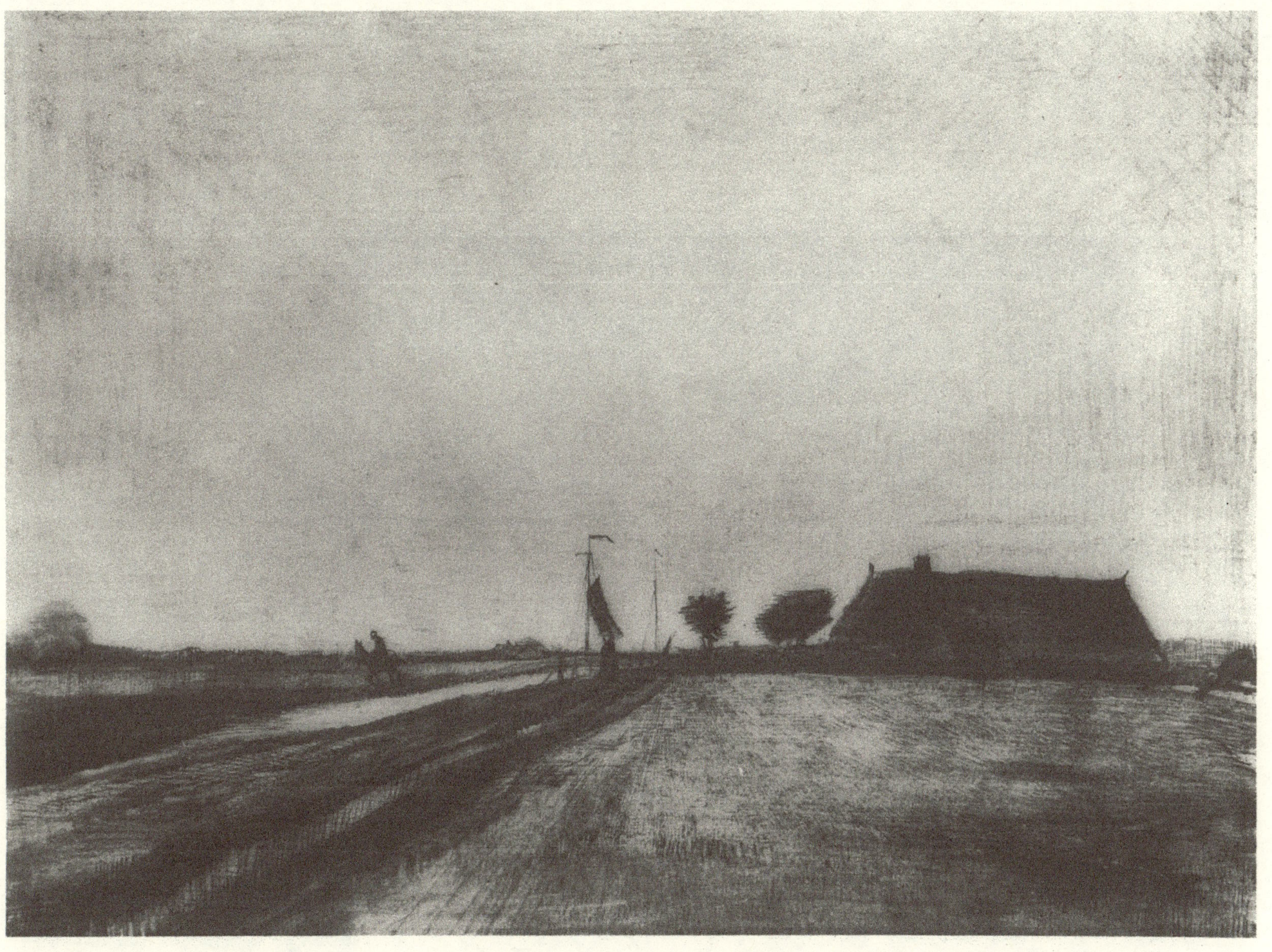

Landscape with canal and sailing boat. 1883. Pen, ink and pencil, washed; 28 × 40 cm. (Photograph: Netherlands Institute for Art History, The Hague.)

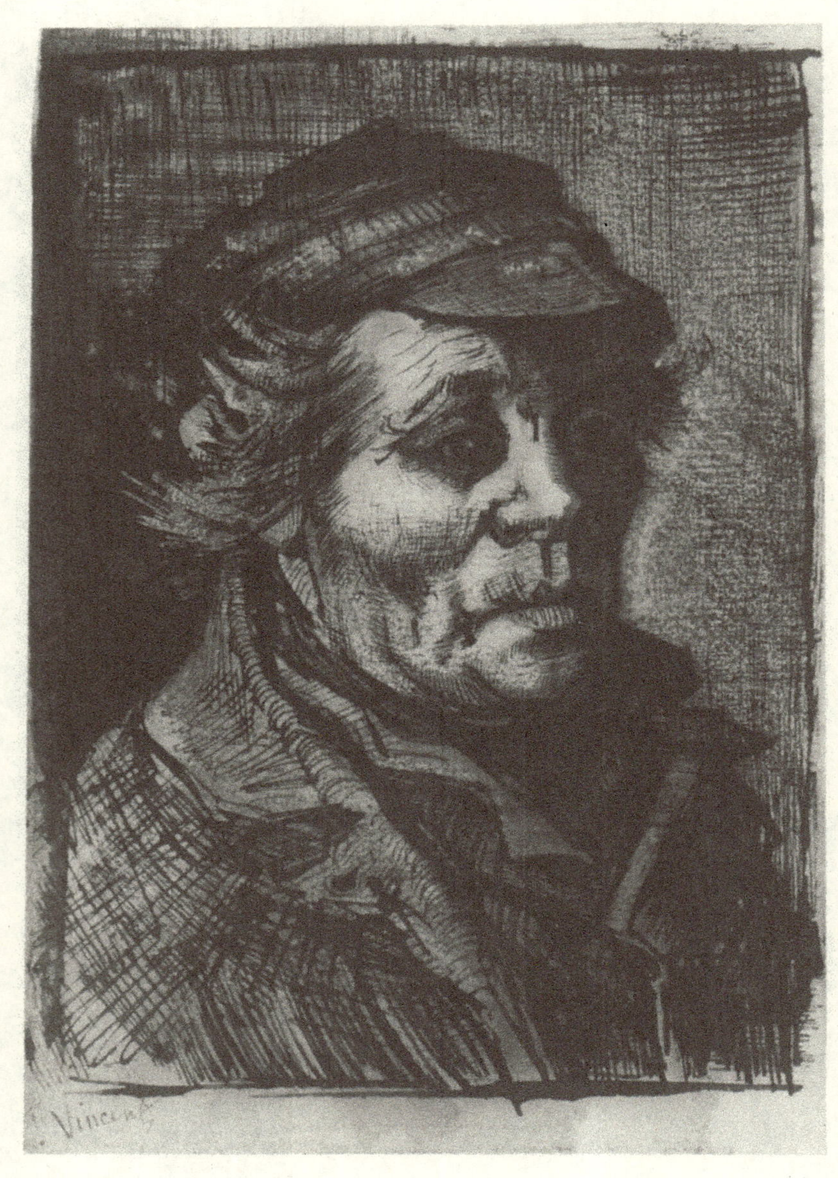

Head of a peasant. 1884. Pen, pencil, brown chalk and black ink, washed; 14.5 × 10.5 cm. (Van Gogh Foundation/National Museum Vincent van Gogh, Amsterdam.)

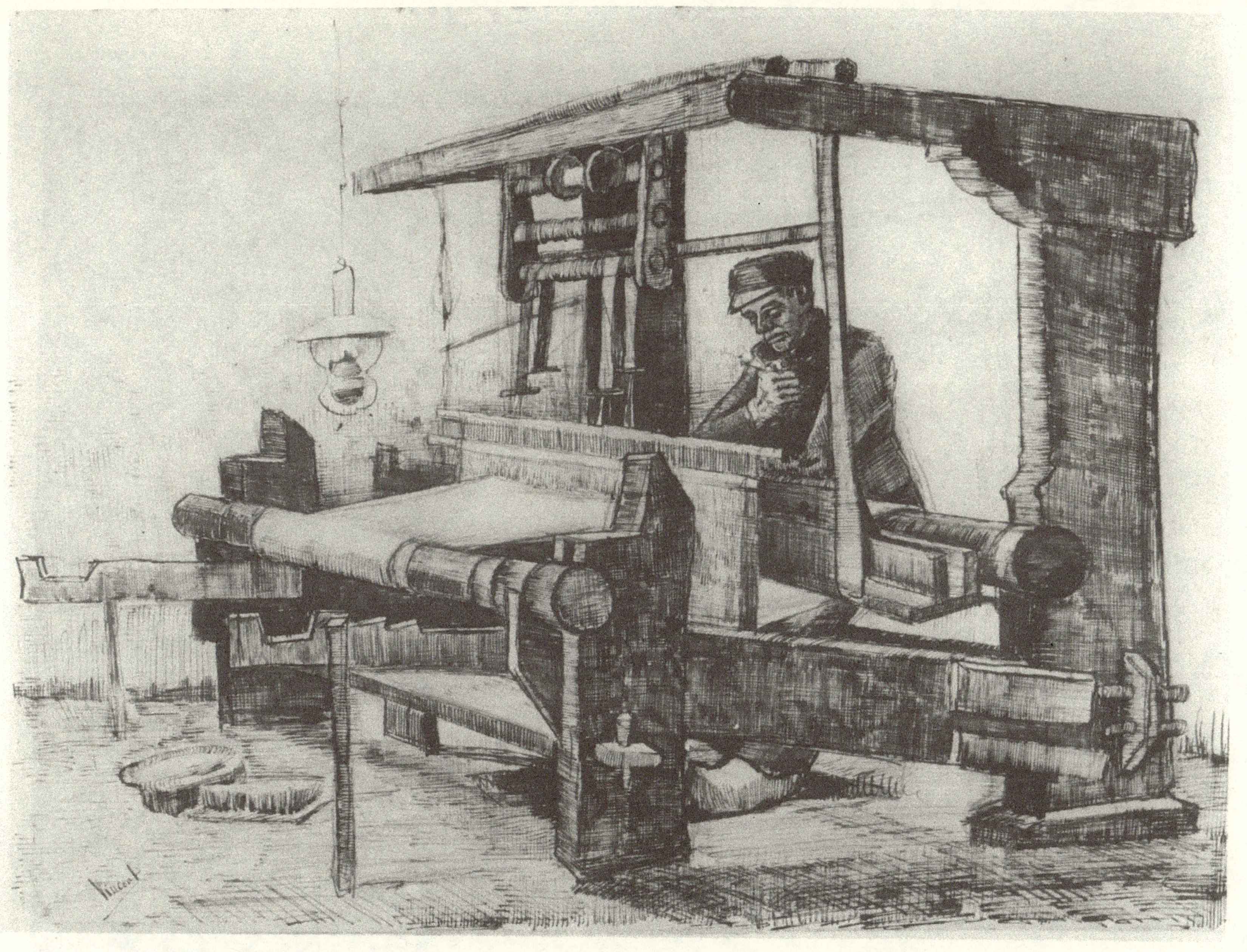

Weaver facing left. 1884. Pen and ink, heightened with white; 30.5 × 40.5 cm. (Van Gogh Foundation/ National Museum Vincent van Gogh, Amsterdam.)

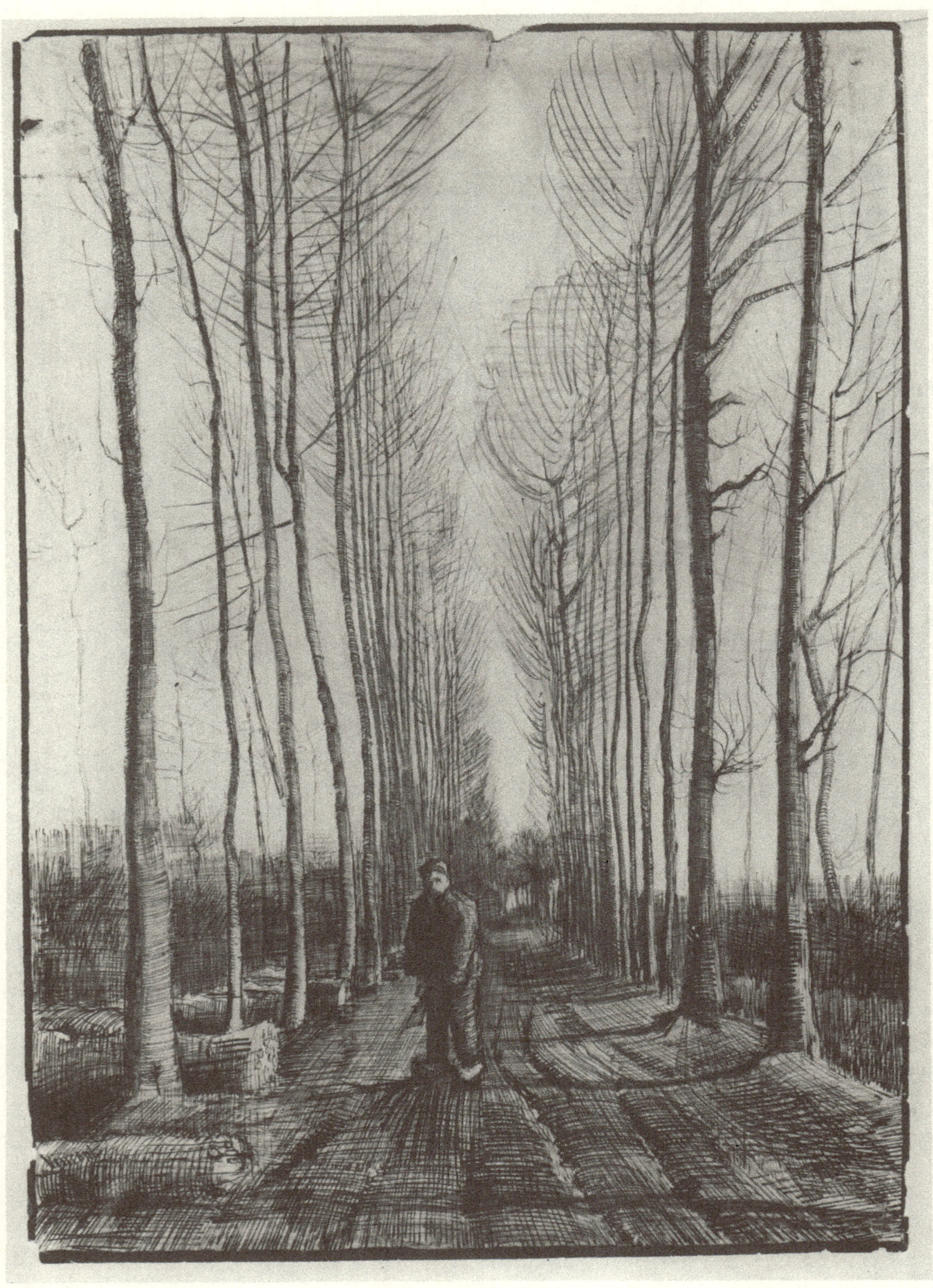

Lane of poplars with one figure. 1884. Pen and ink; 54 × 39 cm. (Van Gogh Foundation/National Museum Vincent van Gogh, Amsterdam.)

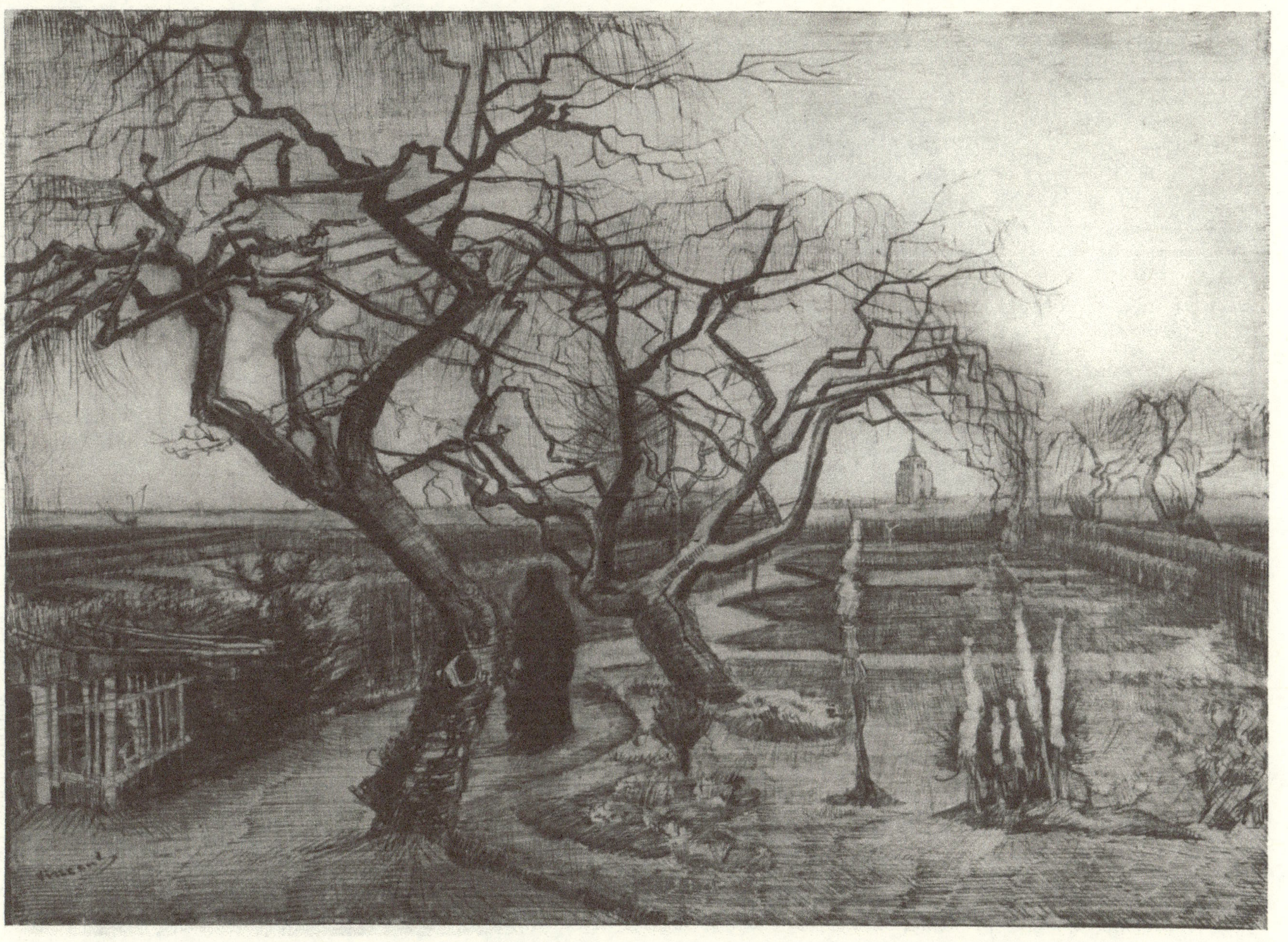

Parsonage garden. 1884. Pencil, pen and ink; 39 × 53 cm. (Van Gogh Foundation/National Museum Vincent van Gogh, Amsterdam.)

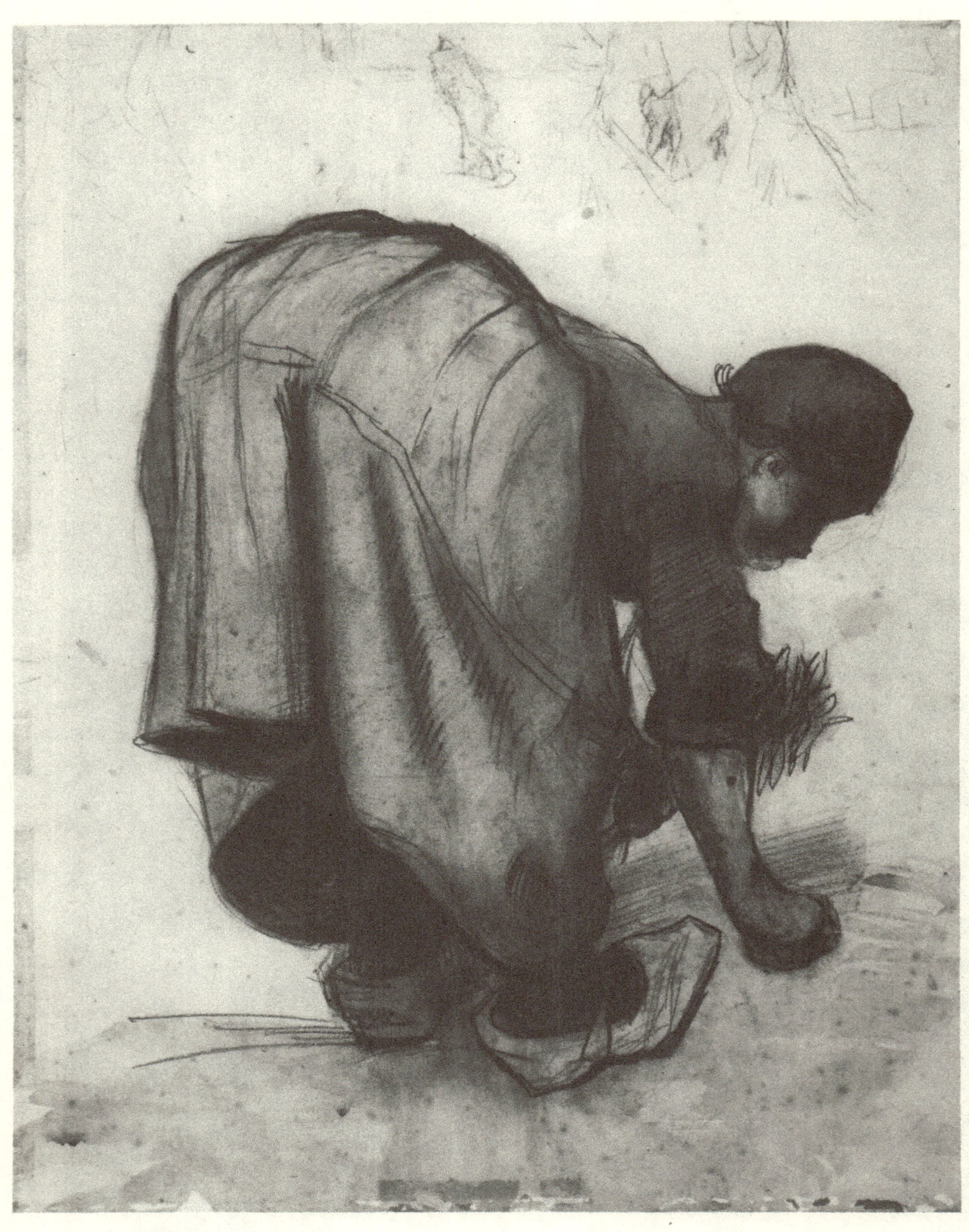

Peasant woman, stooping, seen from the back. 1885. Black chalk, washed; 52.5 × 43.5 cm. (State Museum Kröller-Müller, Otterlo, The Netherlands.)

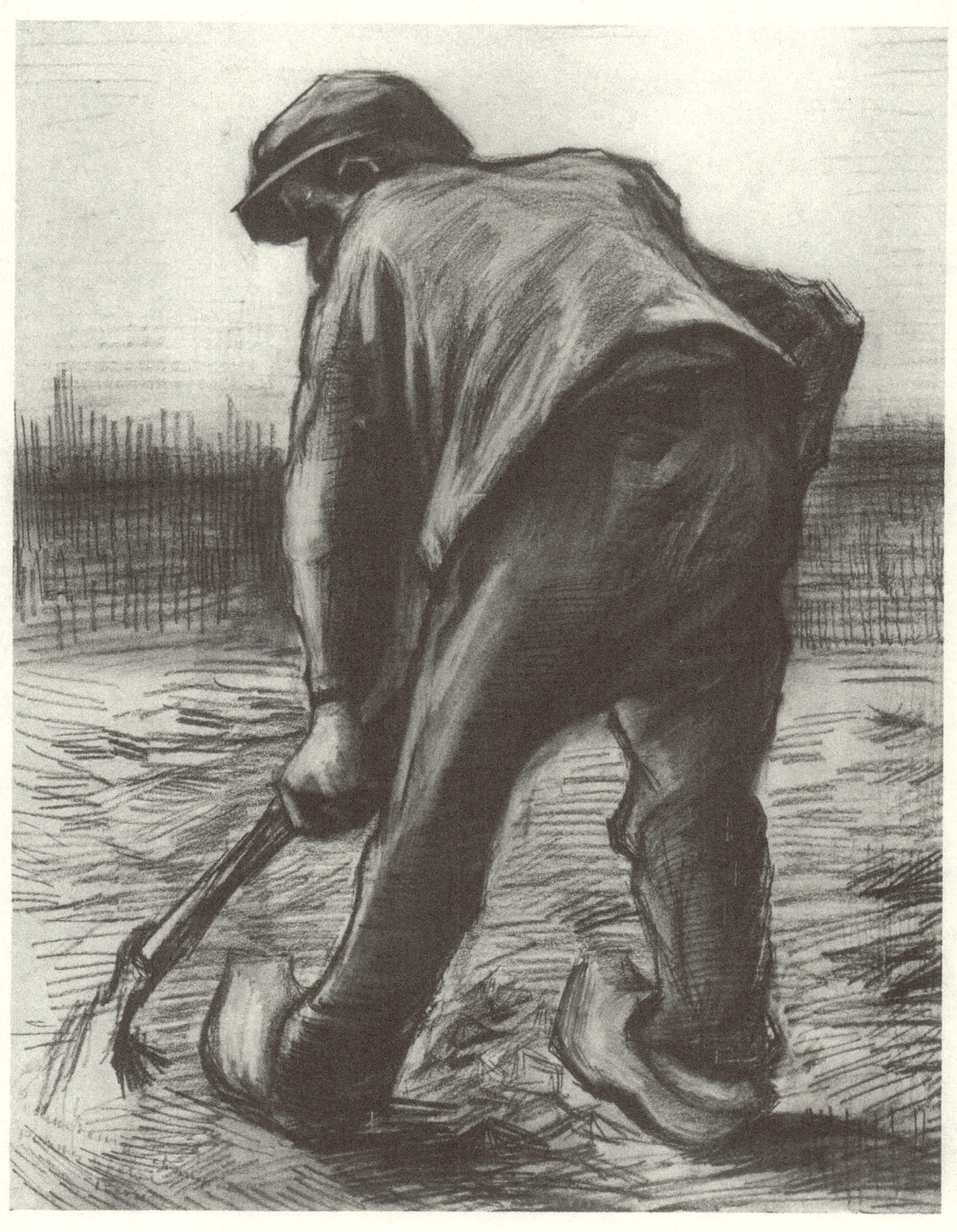

Peasant, digging, seen from the back. 1885. Black chalk; 53 × 41 cm. (Van Gogh Foundation/ National Museum Vincent van Gogh, Amsterdam.)

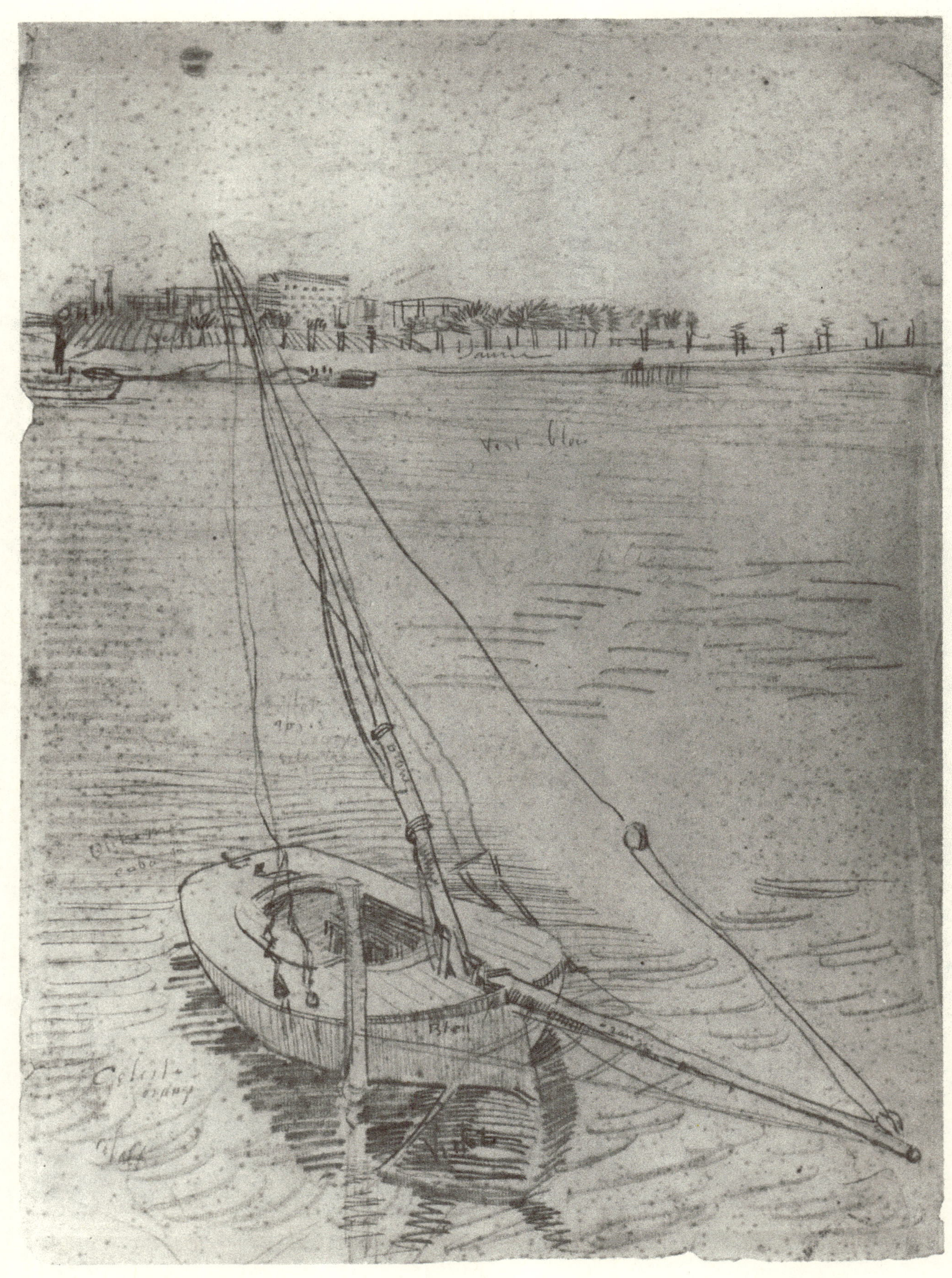

Sailboat on the Seine at Asnières. 1887. Pencil; 53.5 × 43.5 cm. (Van Gogh Foundation/National Museum Vincent van Gogh, Amsterdam.)

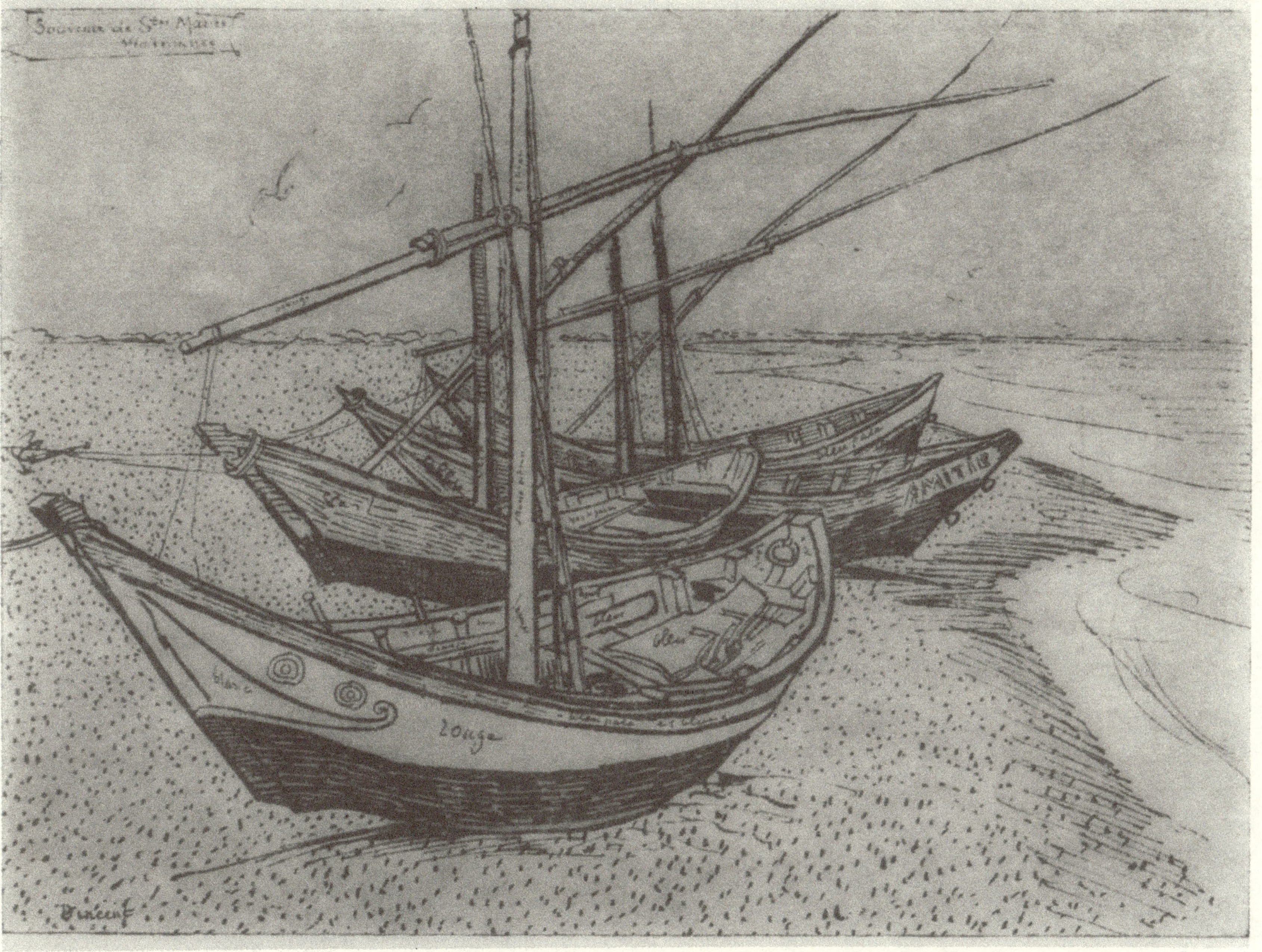

Fishing boats on the beach. 1888. Reed pen and ink; 39.5 × 53.5 cm. (Private collection. Photograph: Netherlands Institute for Art History, The Hague.)

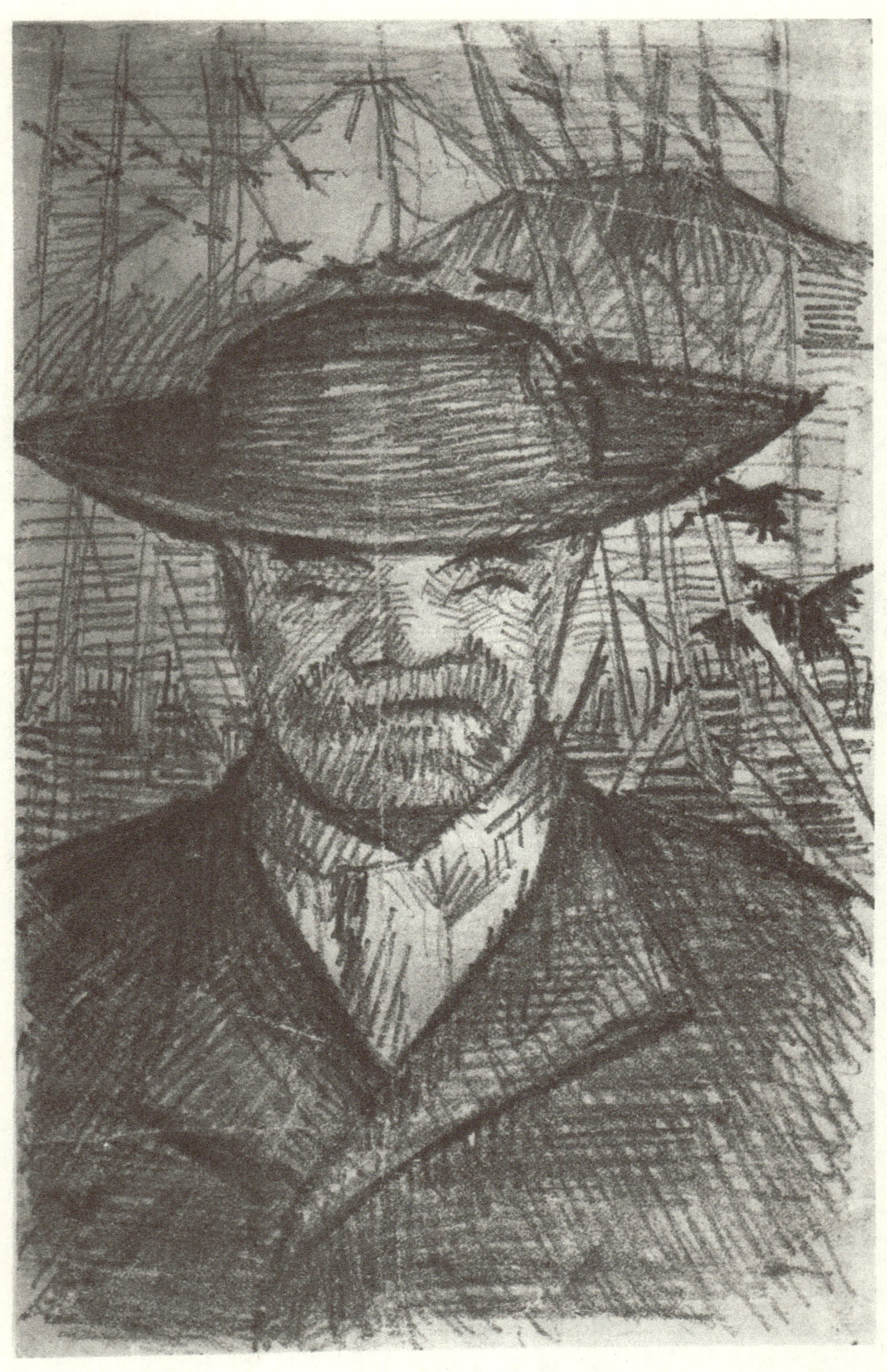

Portrait of Père Tanguy. 1887/88. Pencil; 21.5 × 13.5 cm. (Van Gogh Foundation/National Museum Vincent van Gogh, Amsterdam.)

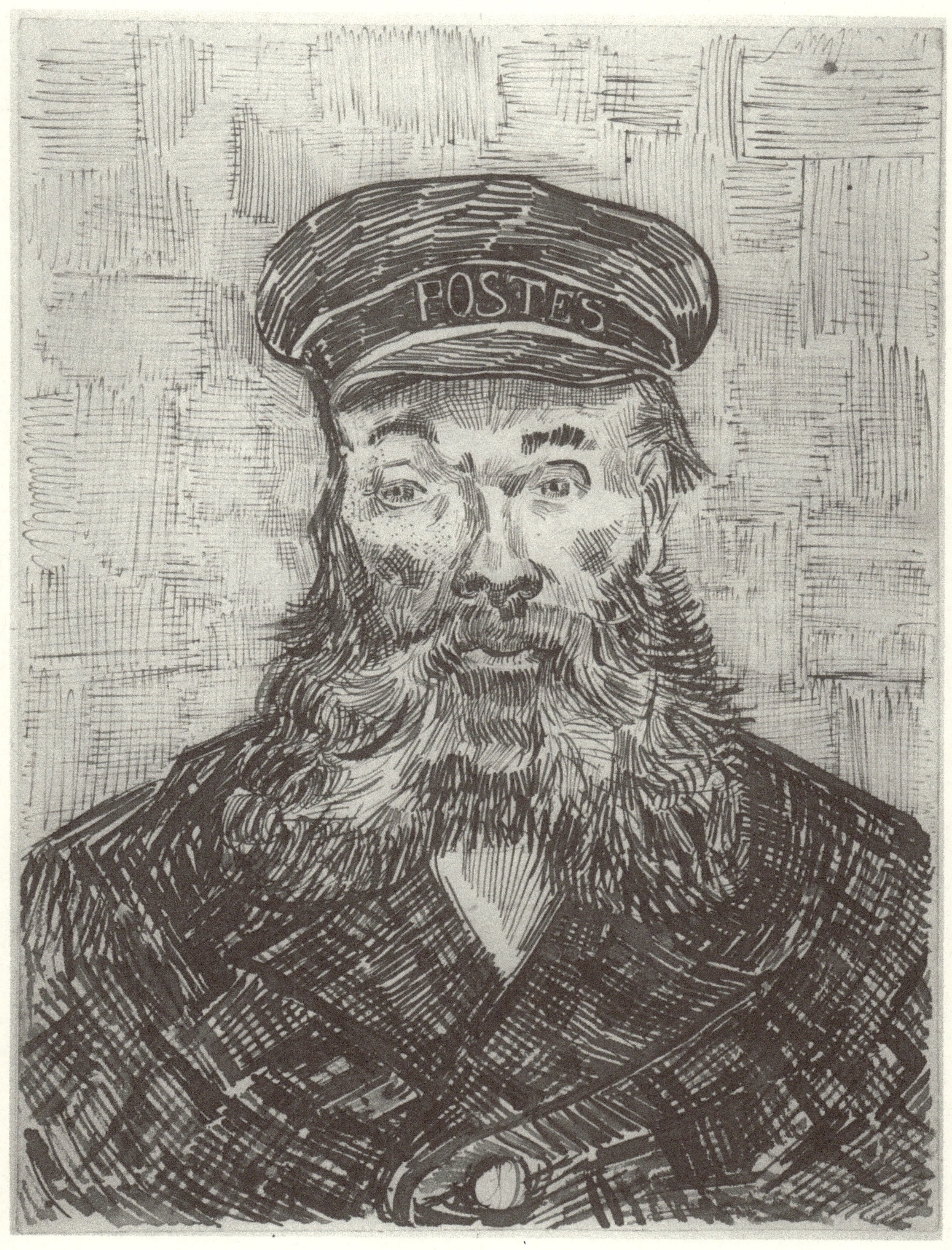

Portrait of Joseph Roulin. 1888. Reed pen, quill pen and brown ink; 31.8 × 24.3 cm. (The J. Paul Getty Museum, Malibu.)

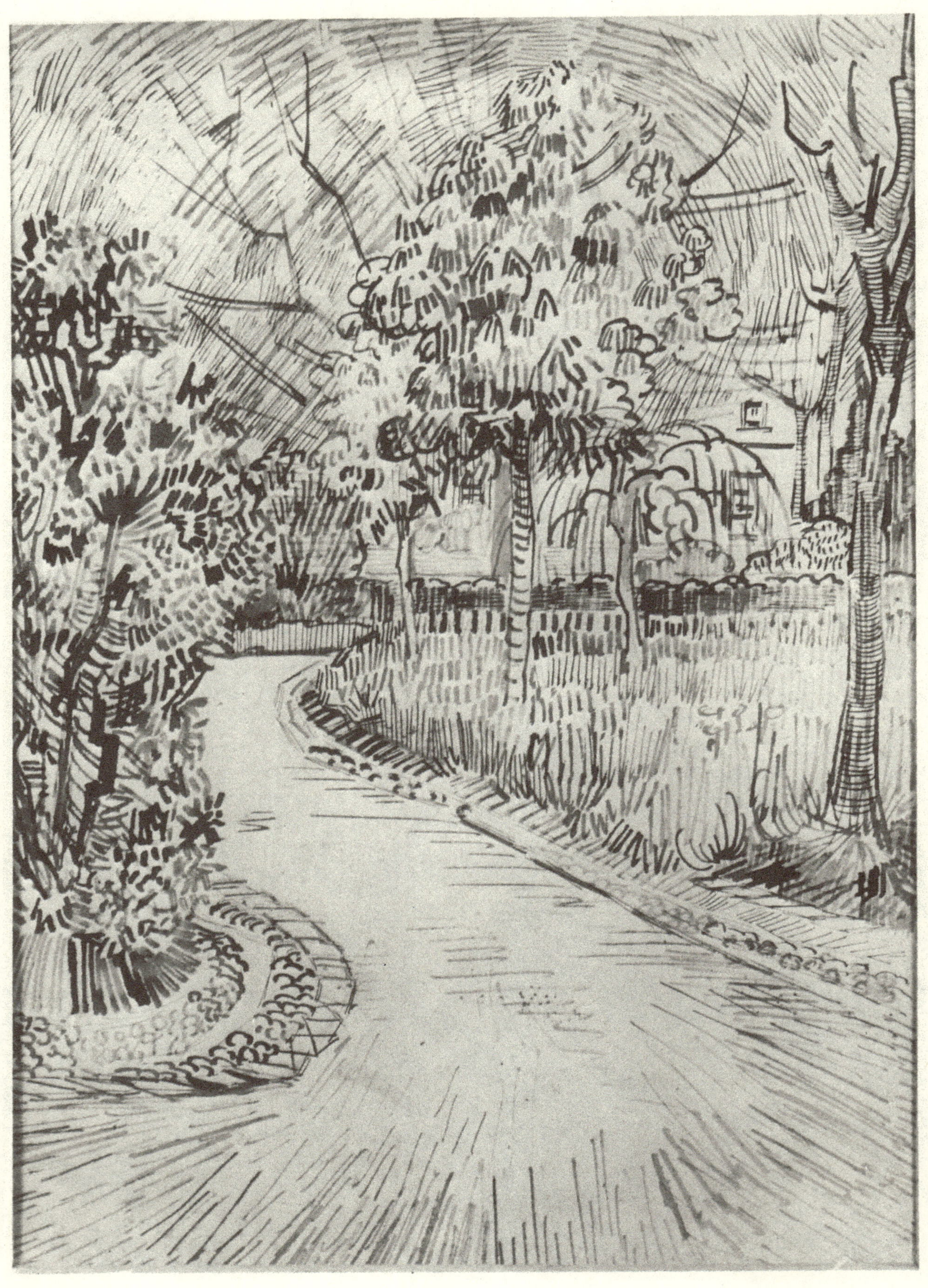

Public garden in Arles, with a corner of the yellow house. 1888. Pen and reed pen; 35 × 26 cm. (Van Gogh Foundation/National Museum Vincent van Gogh, Amsterdam.)

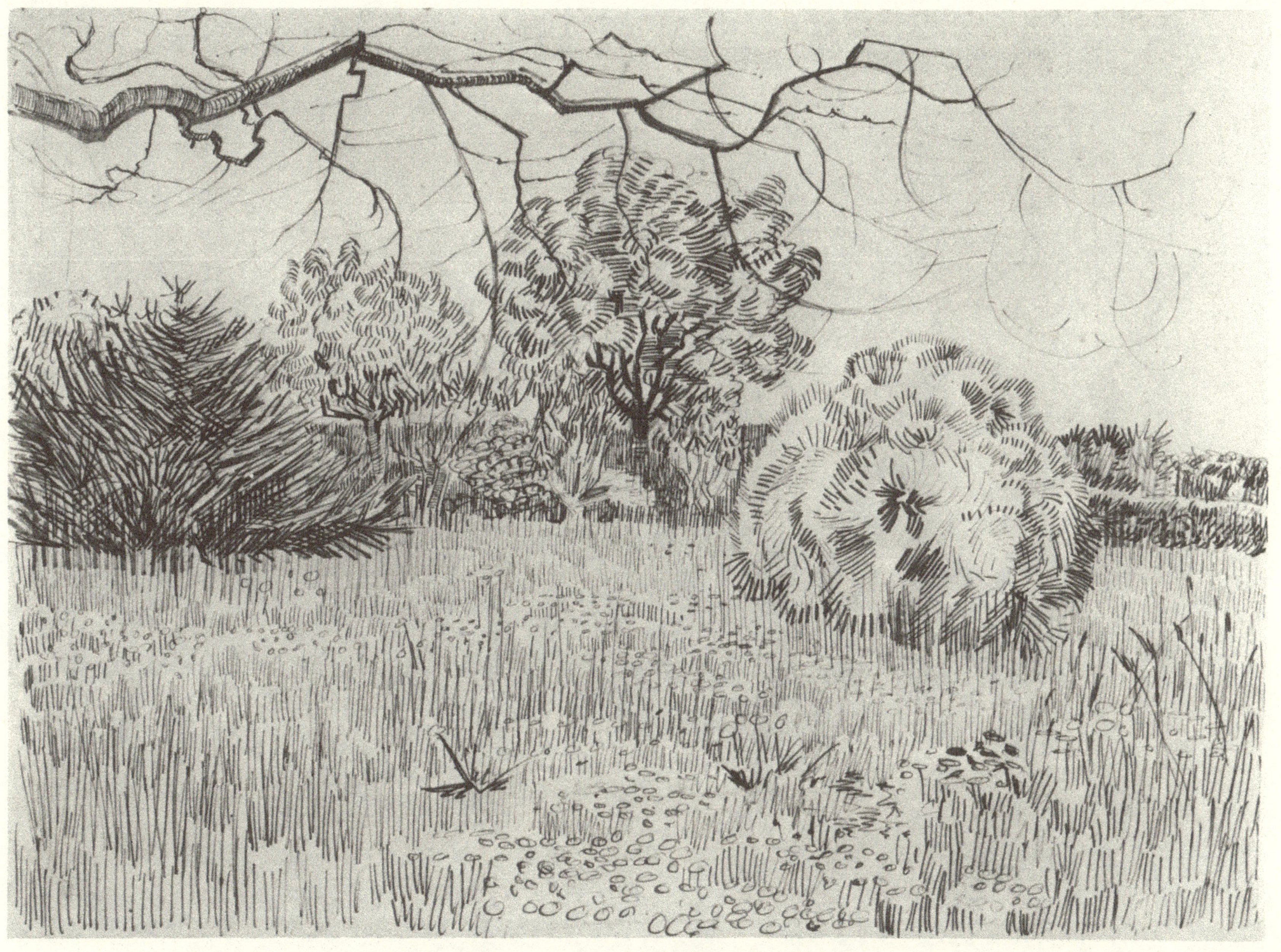

Field of grass with a round clipped shrub. 1888. Pencil, reed pen and brown ink; 25.5 × 34.5 cm. (Van Gogh Foundation/National Museum Vincent van Gogh, Amsterdam.)

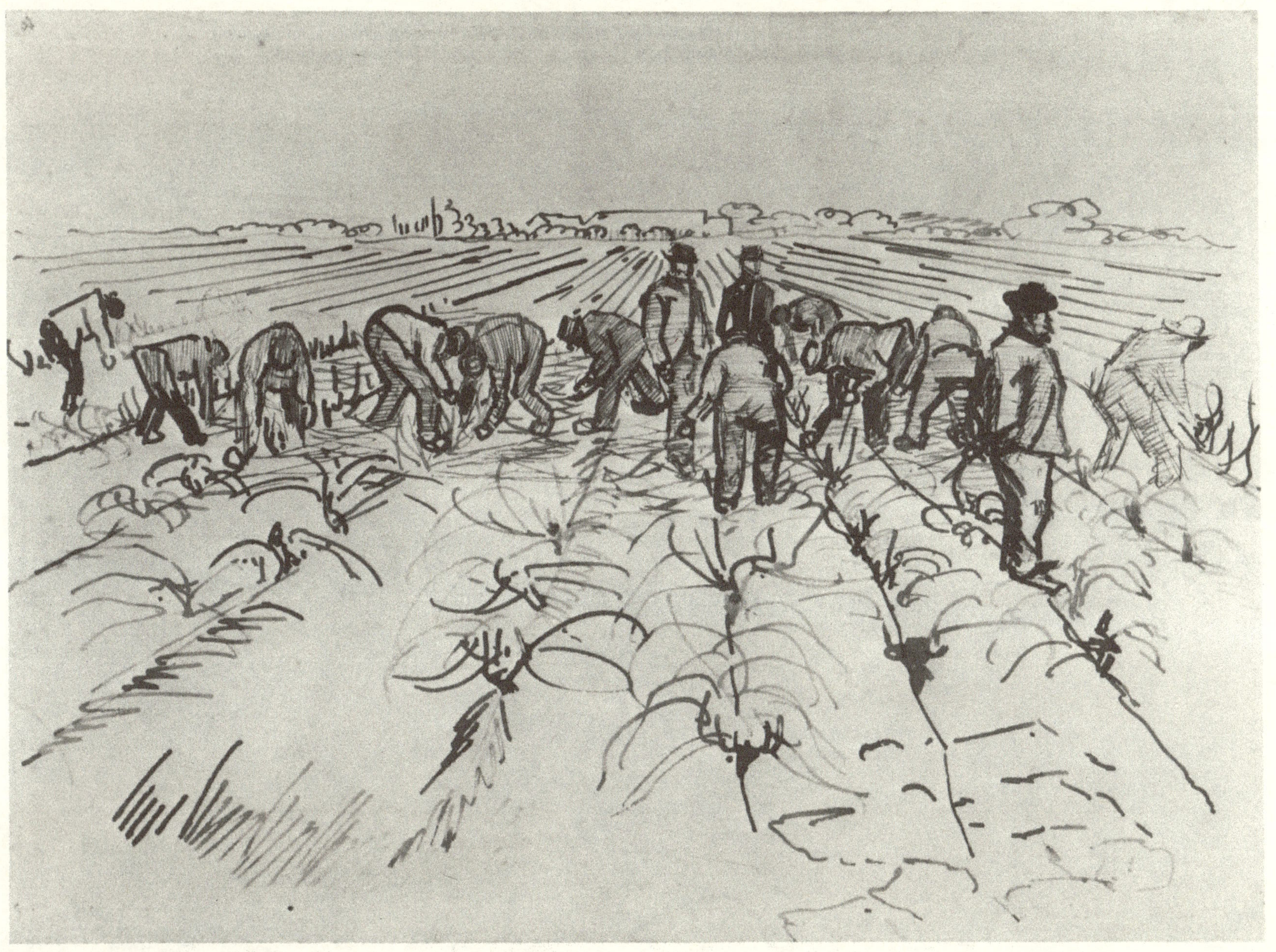

Farmers working in a field. 1888. Reed pen and ink; 26 × 34.5 cm. (Van Gogh Foundation/National Museum Vincent van Gogh, Amsterdam.)

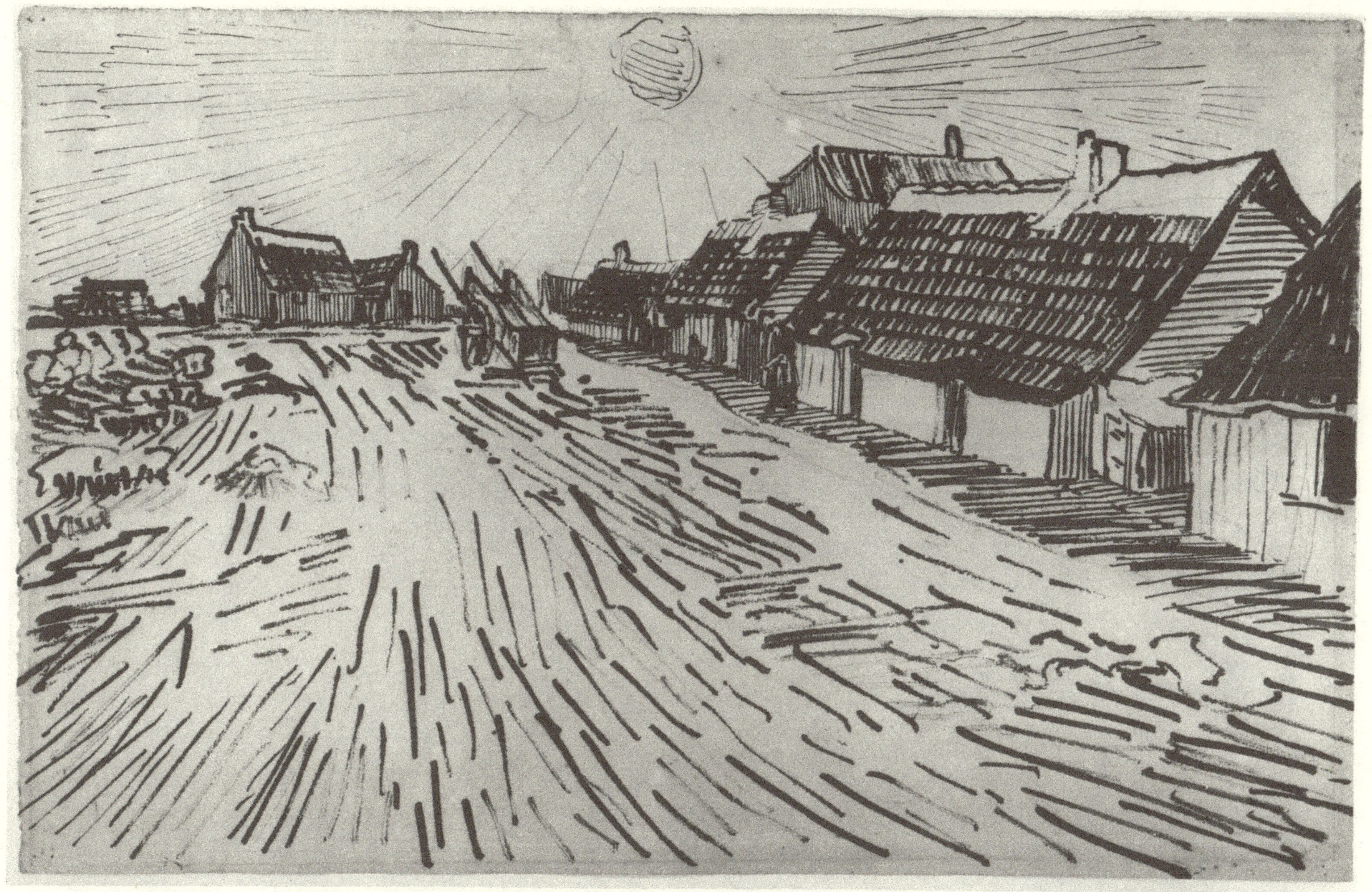

Row of cottages in Saintes-Maries. 1888. Reed pen and ink; 30.5 × 47 cm. (Van Gogh Foundation/National Museum Vincent van Gogh, Amsterdam.)

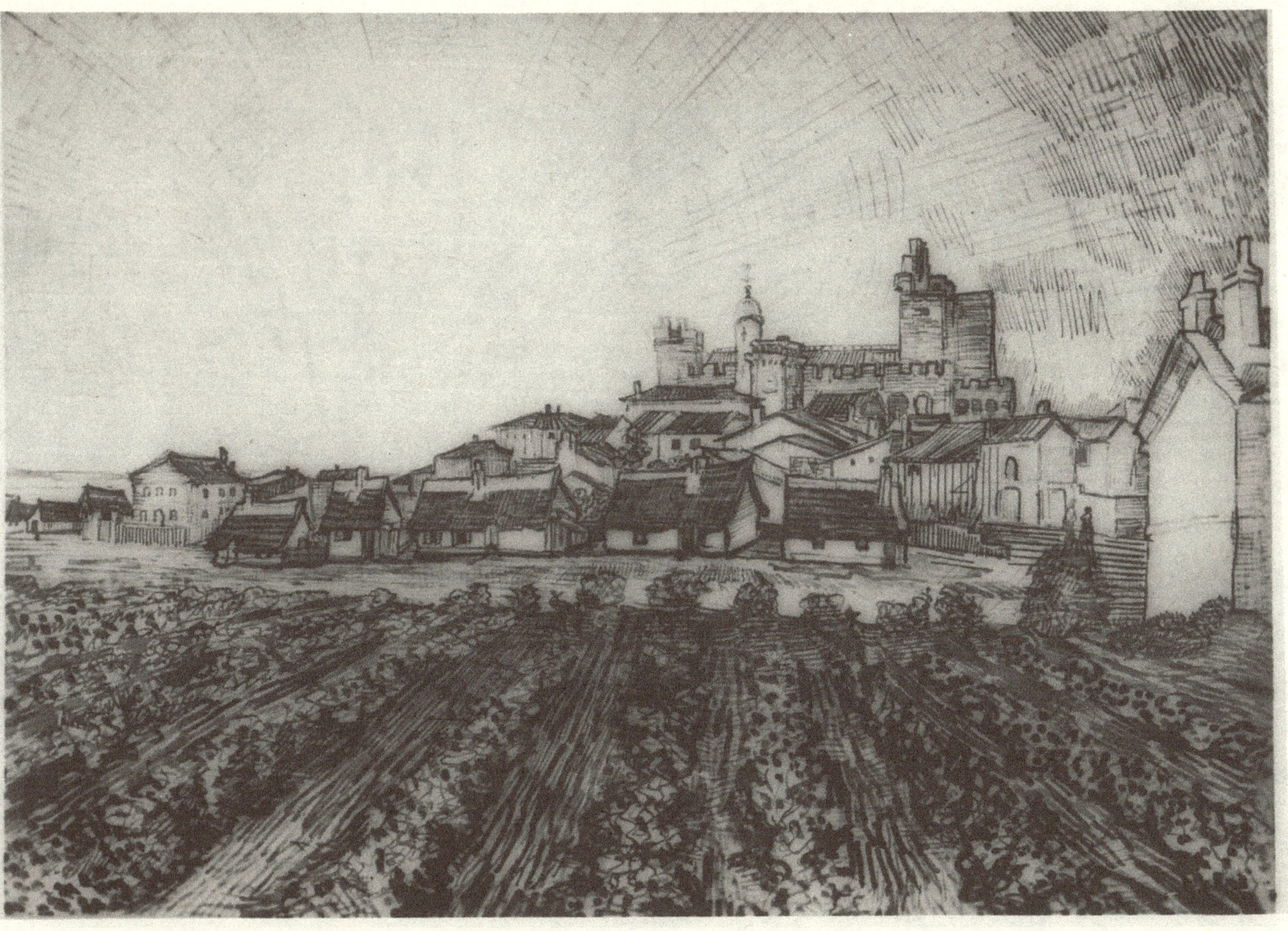

View of Saintes-Maries. 1888. Pen and ink; 43 × 60 cm. (Private collection. Photograph: Netherlands Institute for Art History, The Hague.)

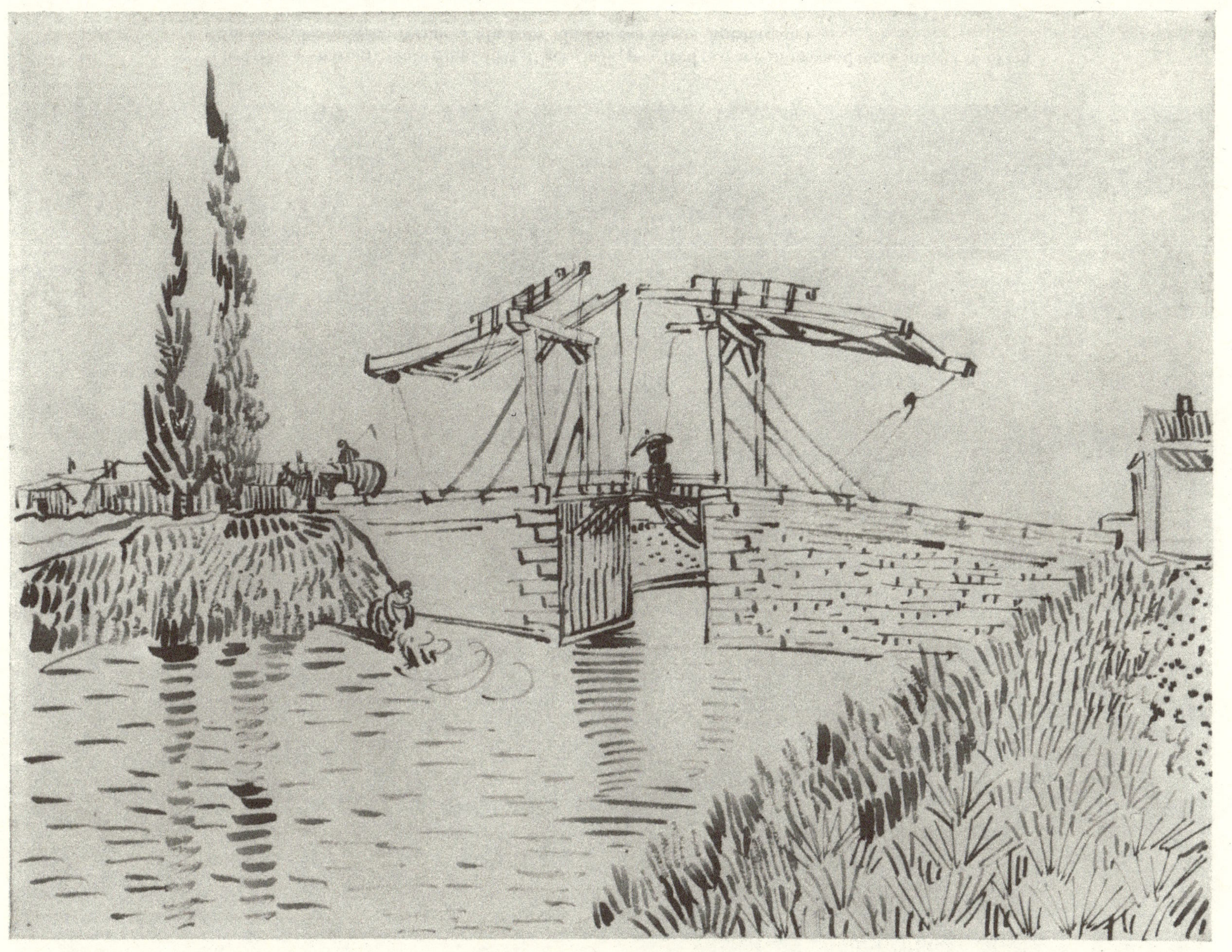

The bridge at Langlois. 1888. Pen and china ink; 24.1 × 31.7 cm. (Los Angeles County Museum of Art, Mr. and Mrs. George Gard de Sylva Collection.)

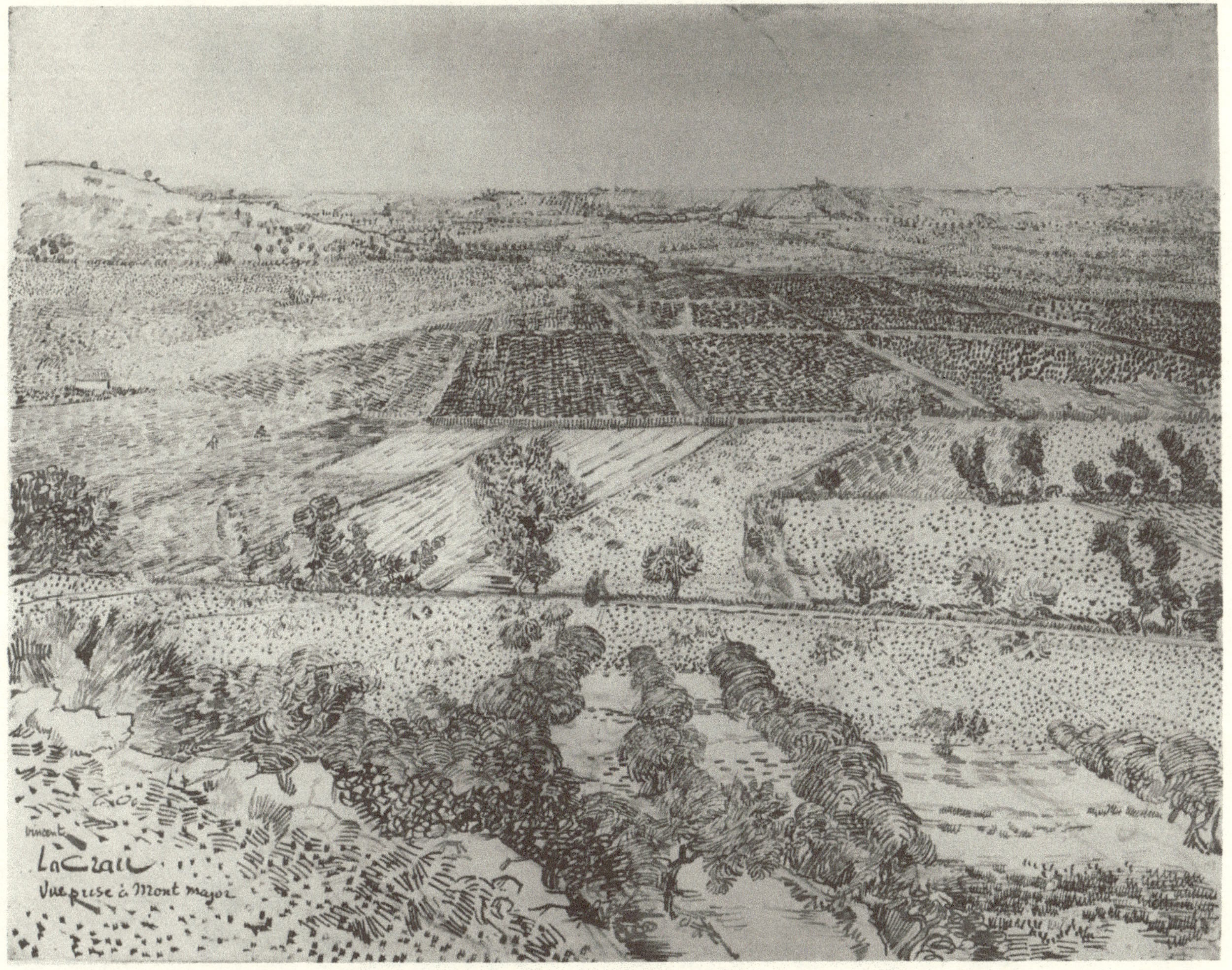

The Crau, seen from Montmajour. 1888. Black chalk, pen, reed pen and brown and black ink; 49 × 61 cm. (Van Gogh Foundation/National Museum Vincent van Gogh, Amsterdam.)

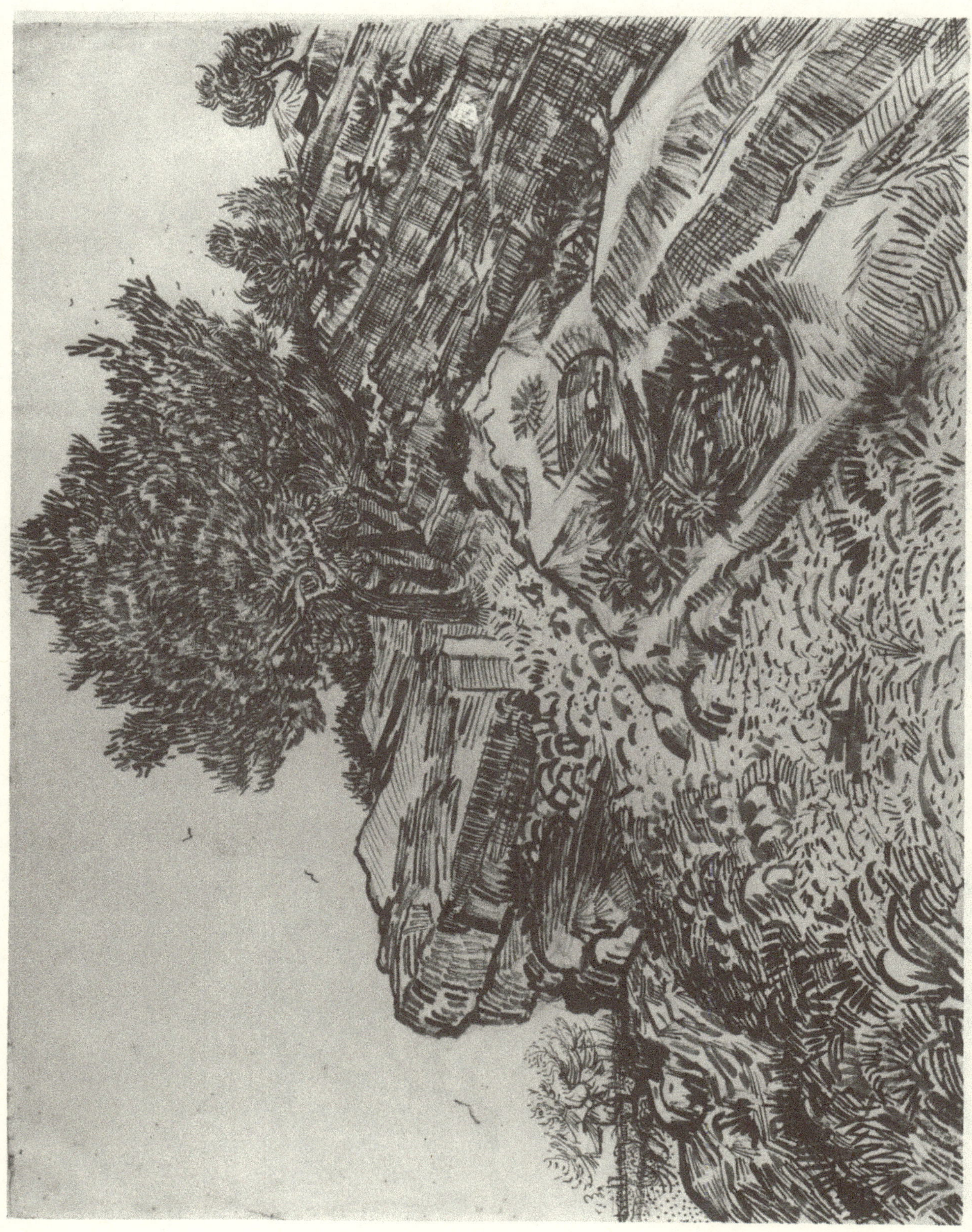

Rocks with trees. 1888. Pencil, pen, reed pen, brush and black ink; 49 × 60 cm. (Van Gogh Foundation/National Museum Vincent van Gogh, Amsterdam.)

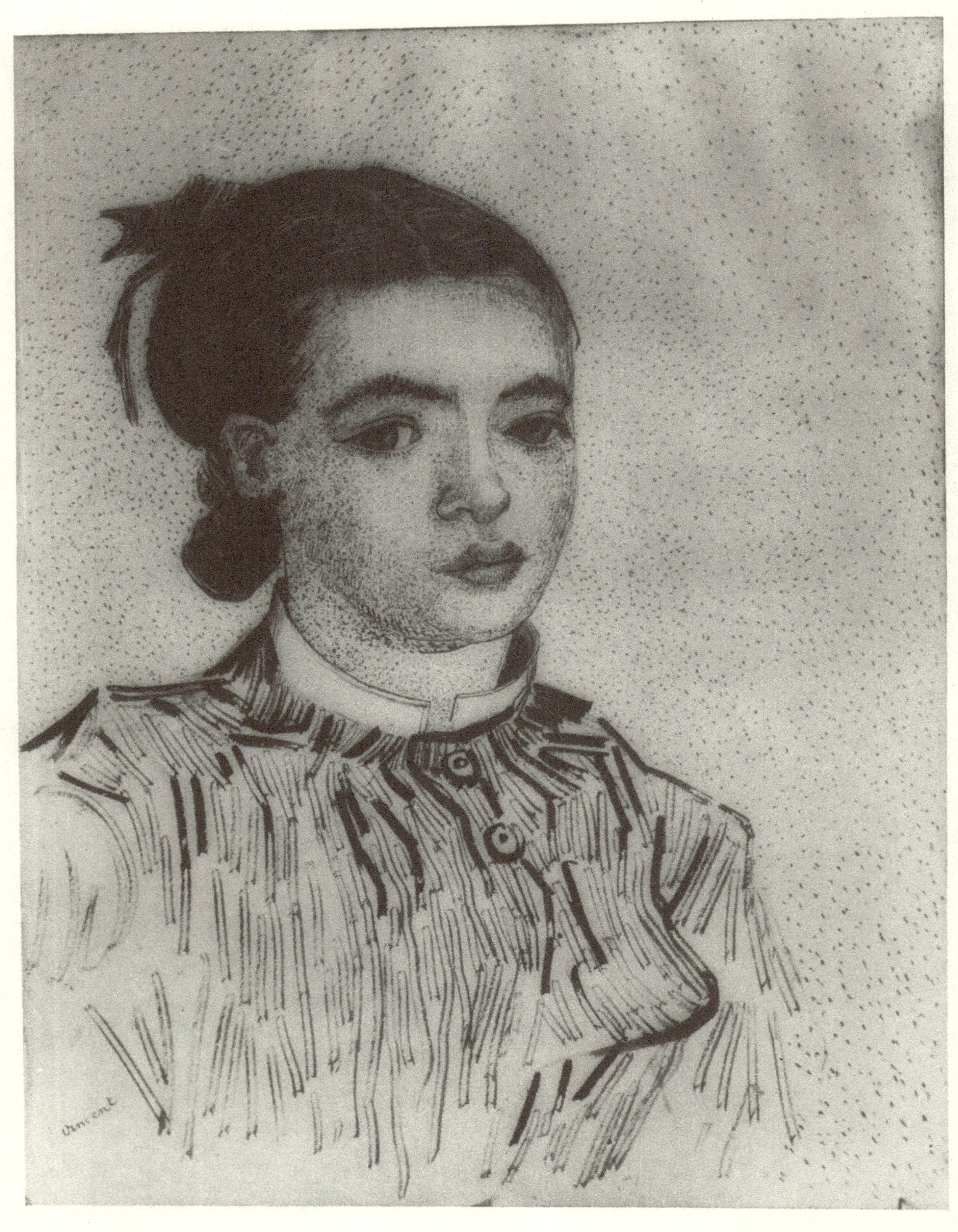

Mousmé, half-figure. 1888. Pen, reed pen and ink; 31.5 × 24 cm. (Private collection. Photograph: Netherlands Institute for Art History, The Hague.)

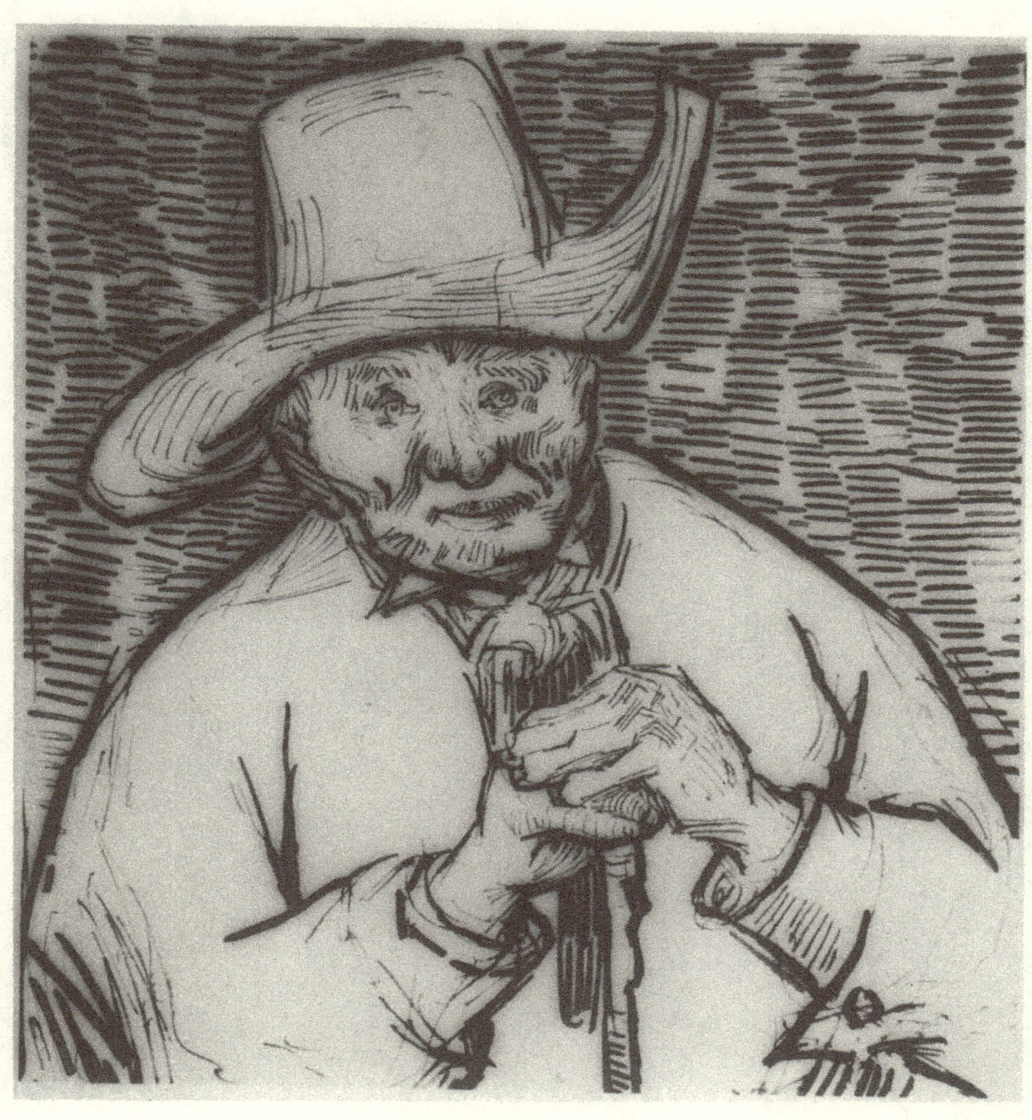

The old peasant Patience Escalier, half-figure. 1888. Reed pen and ink; 14 × 13 cm. (Private collection. Photograph: Netherlands Institute for Art History, The Hague.)

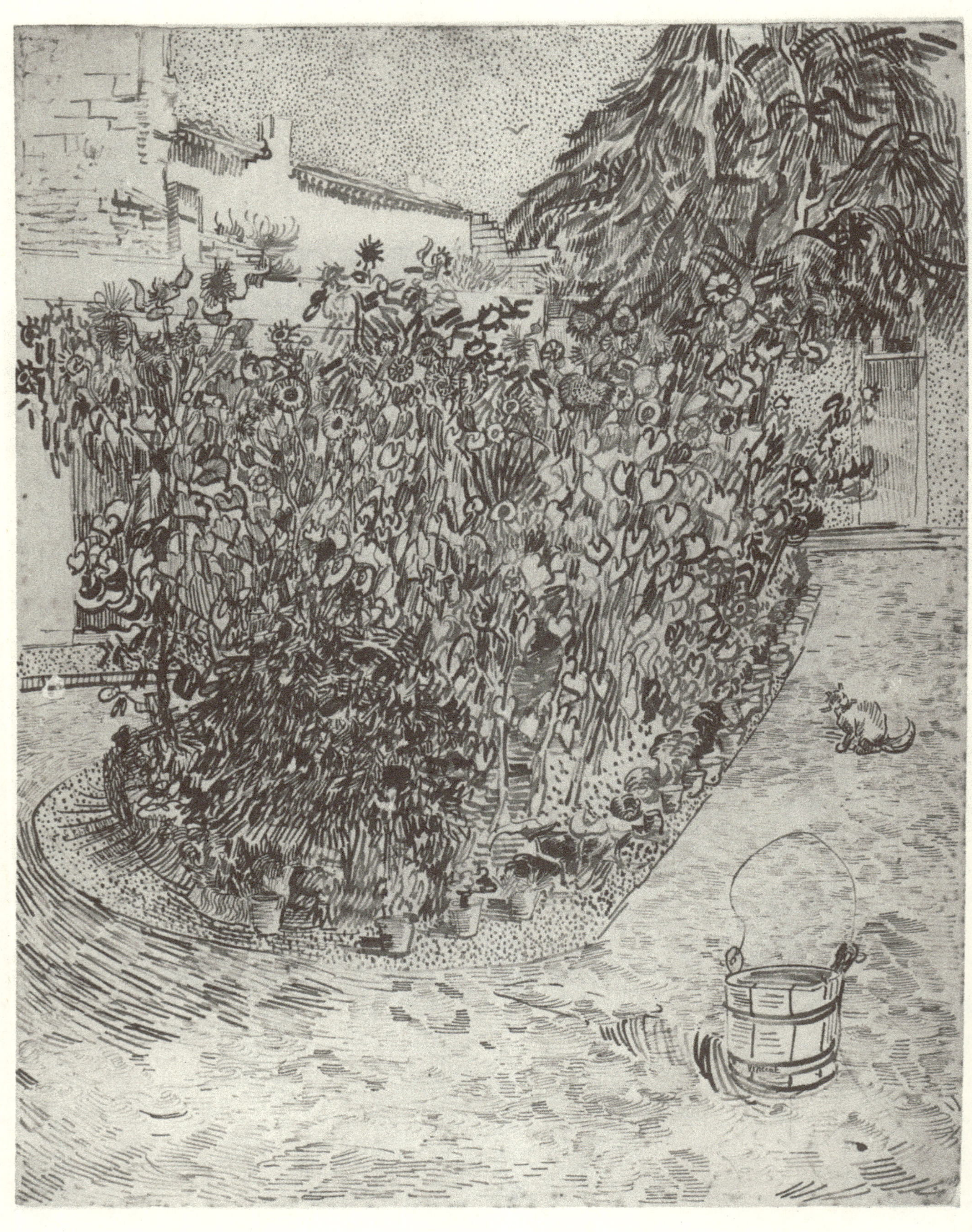

Garden with sunflowers. 1888. Pencil, reed pen and brown ink; 60 × 48.5 cm. (Van Gogh Foundation/National Museum Vincent van Gogh, Amsterdam.)

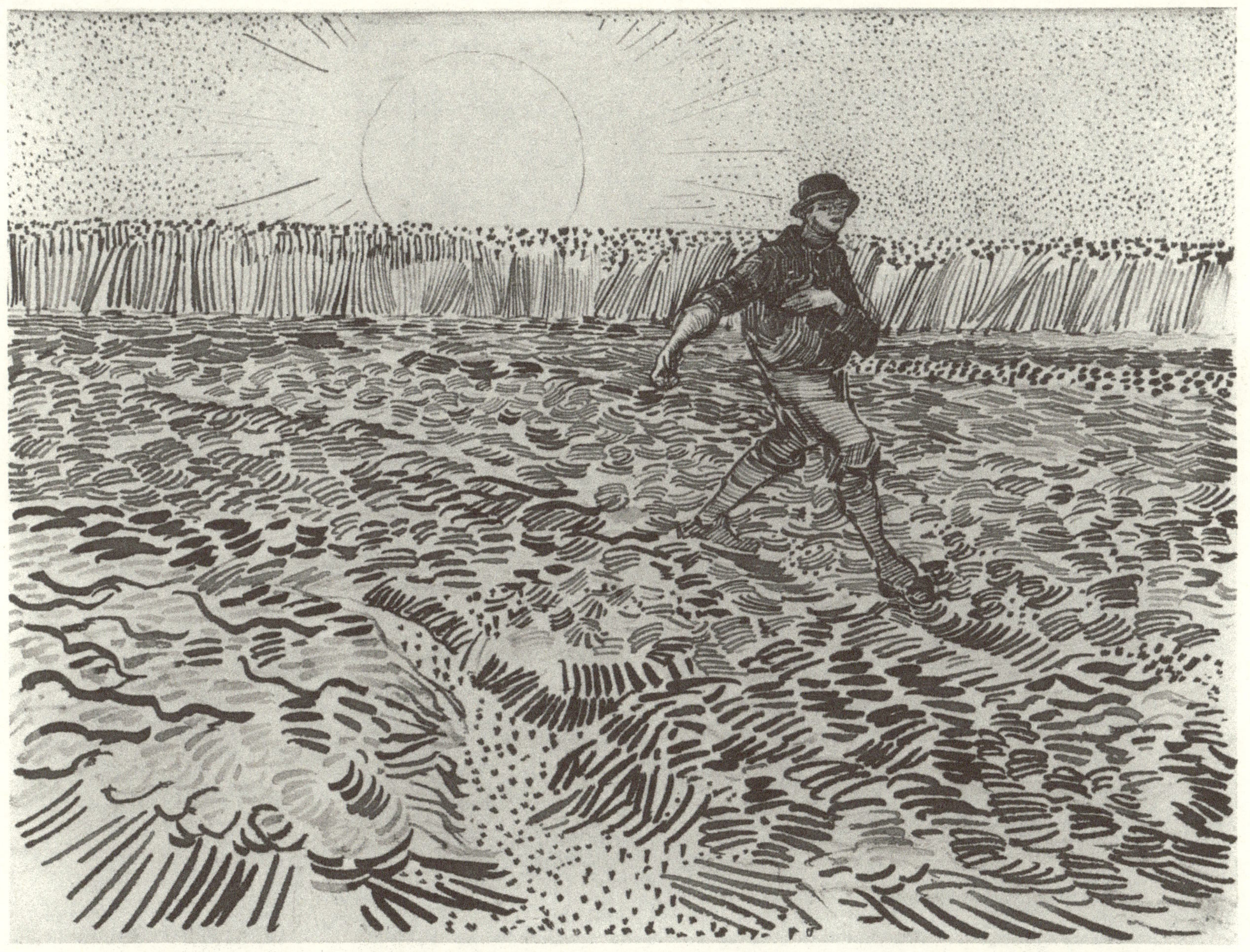

Sower with setting sun. 1888. Reed pen and ink; 24.5 × 32 cm. (Van Gogh Foundation/National Museum Vincent van Gogh, Amsterdam.)

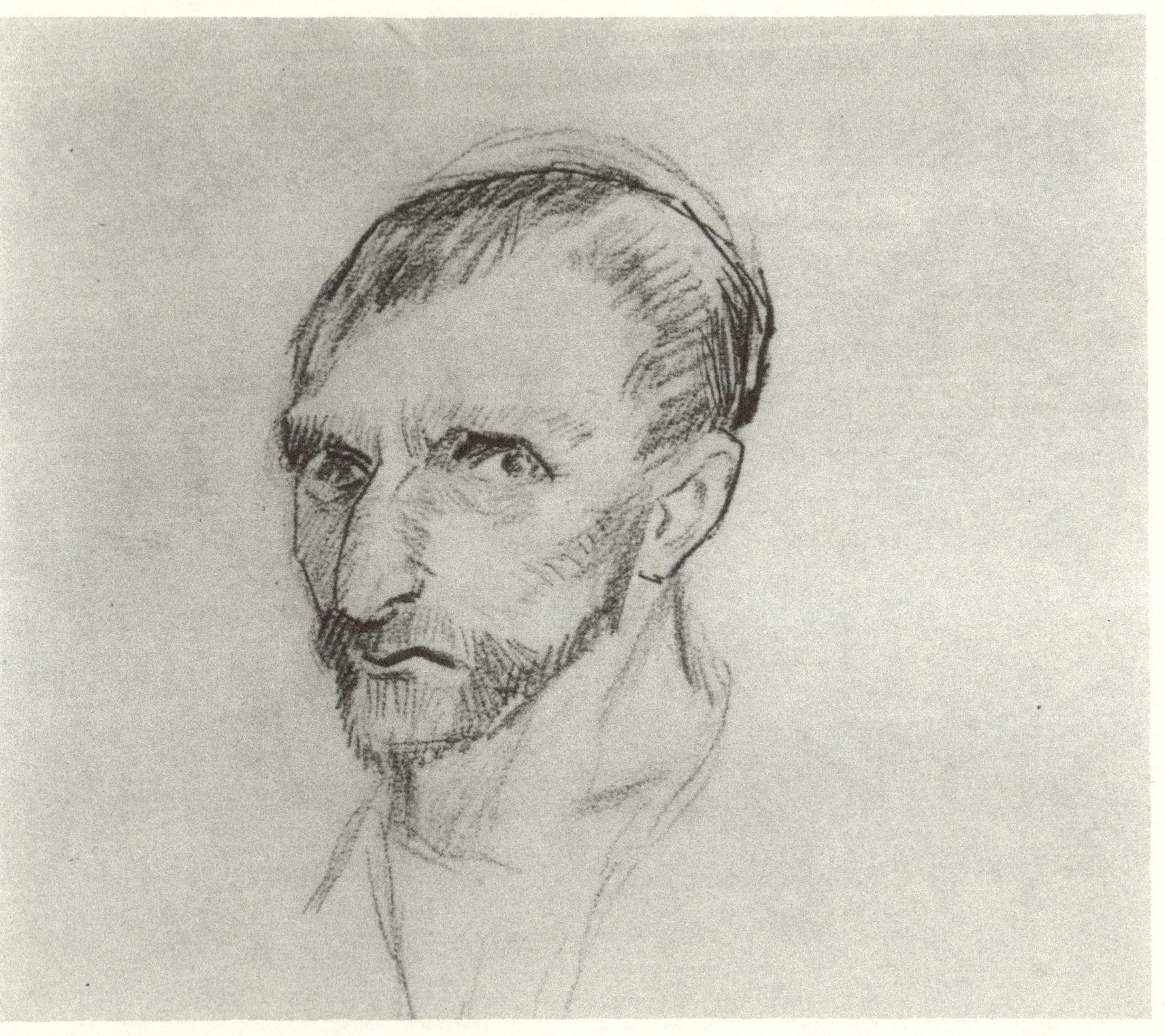

Self-portrait. 1887. Pencil; 19.3 × 21 cm. (Van Gogh Foundation/National Museum Vincent van Gogh, Amsterdam.)

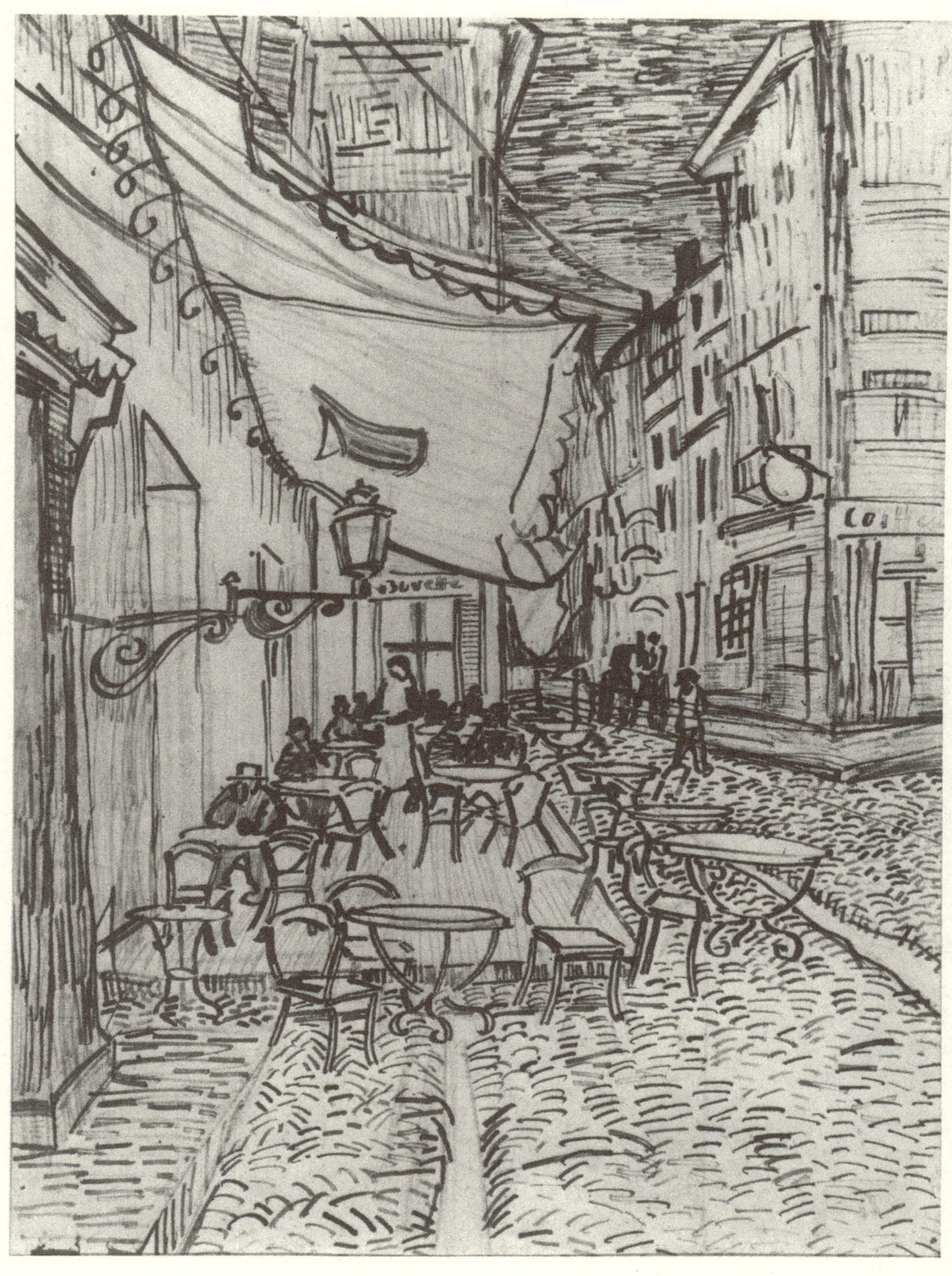

Café terrace at night. 1888. Reed pen and ink over pencil; 62 × 47 cm. (Dallas Museum of Art, The Wendy and Emery Reves Collection.)

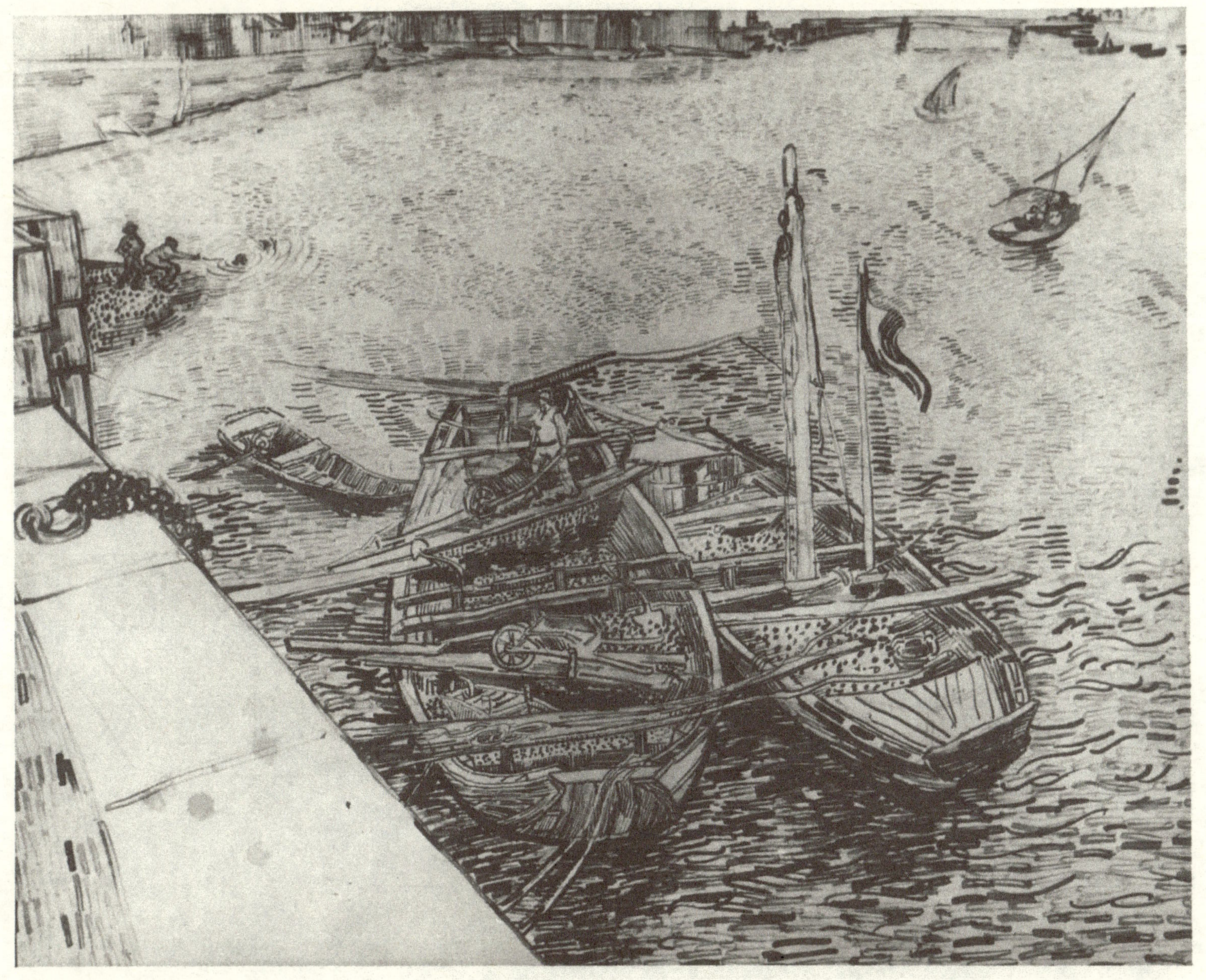

Sand barges. 1888. Pen, reed pen and ink; 48 × 62.5 cm. (Cooper-Hewitt Museum, Smithsonian Institution/Art Resource, gift of Edith Wetmore.)

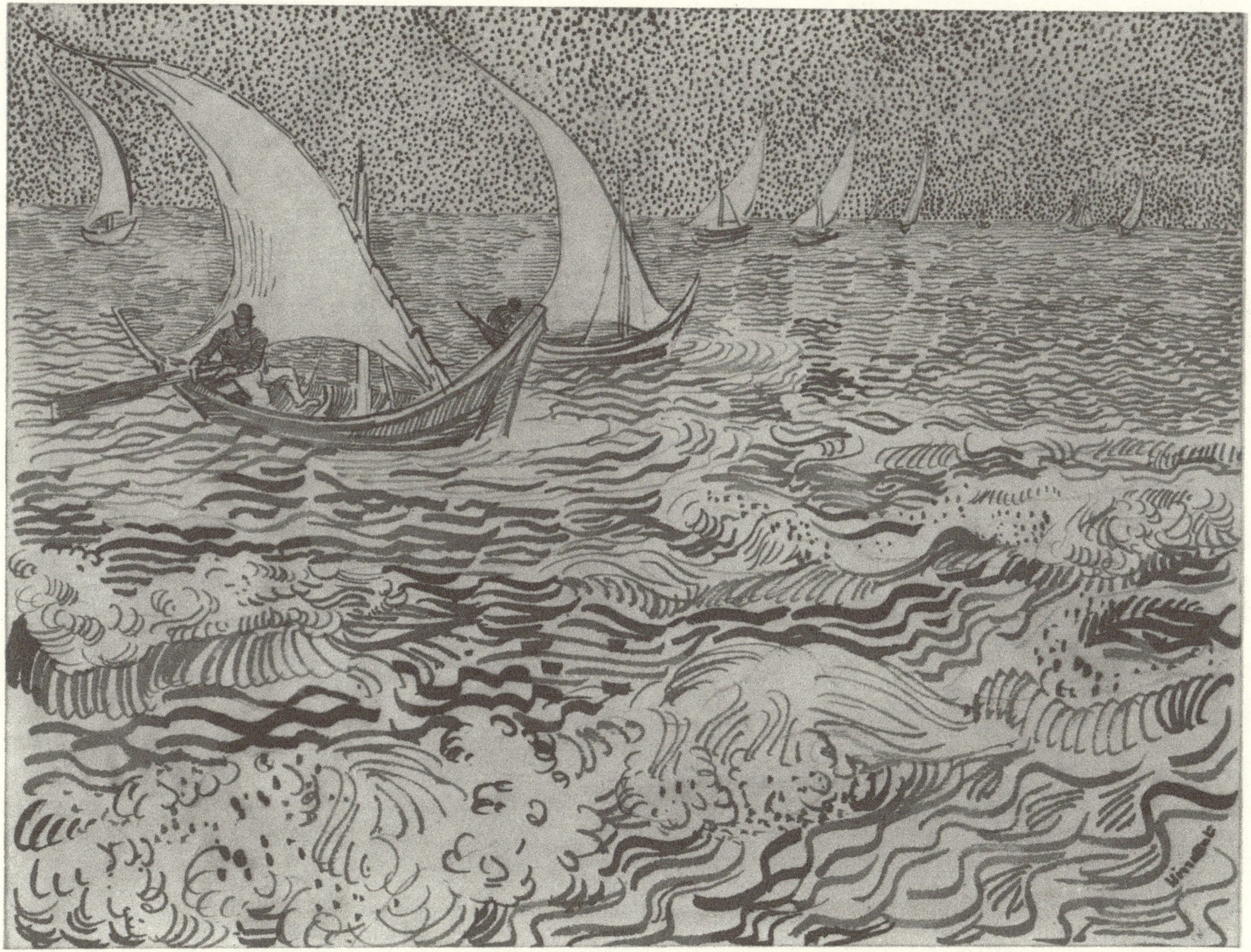

Fishing boats at sea. 1888. Reed pen and ink; 24 × 31.5 cm. (Musée d'Art Moderne, Brussels.)

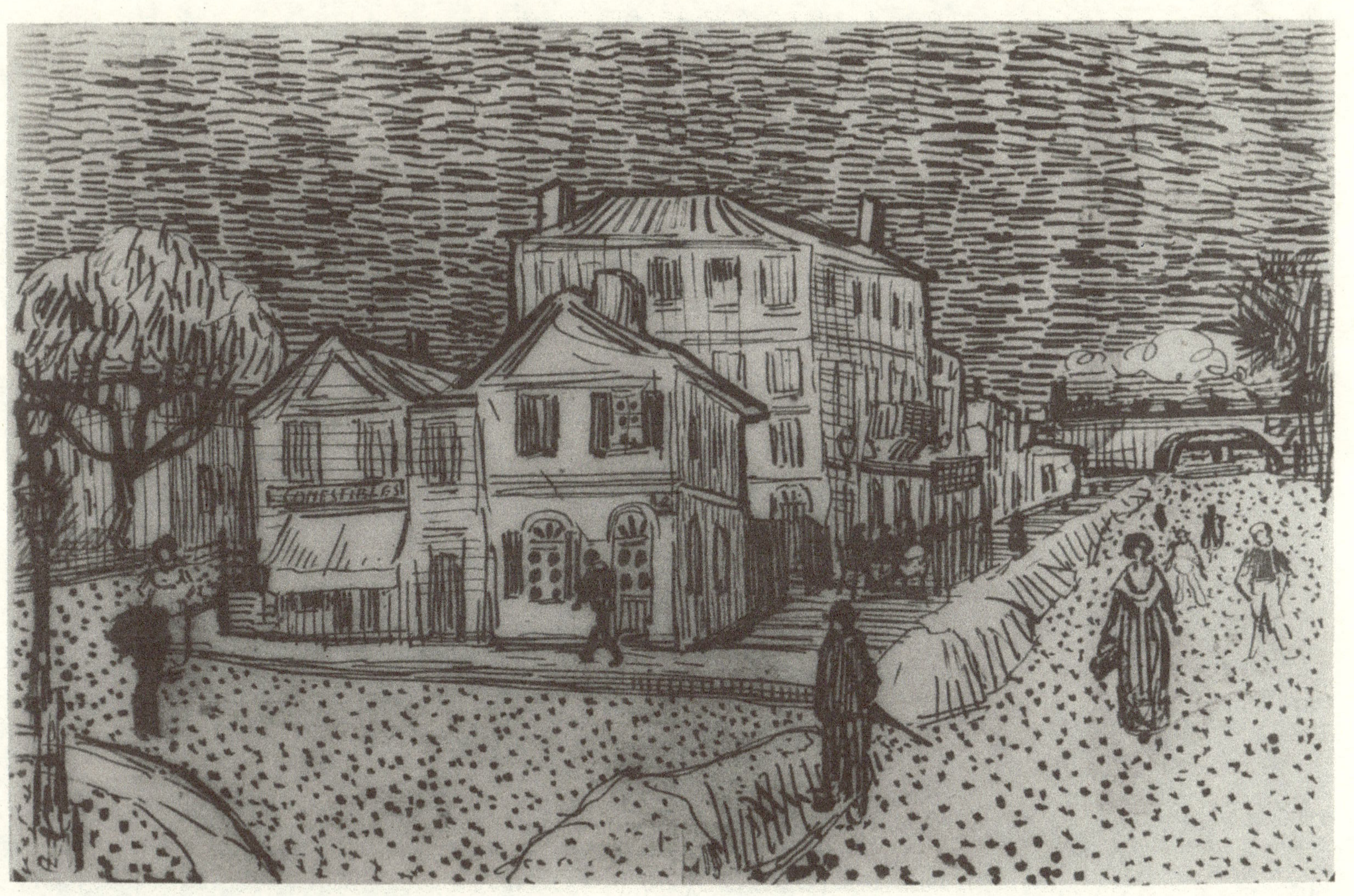

Vincent's house. 1888. Pen and ink; 13 × 20.5 cm. (Private collection. Photograph: Netherlands Institute for Art History, The Hague.)

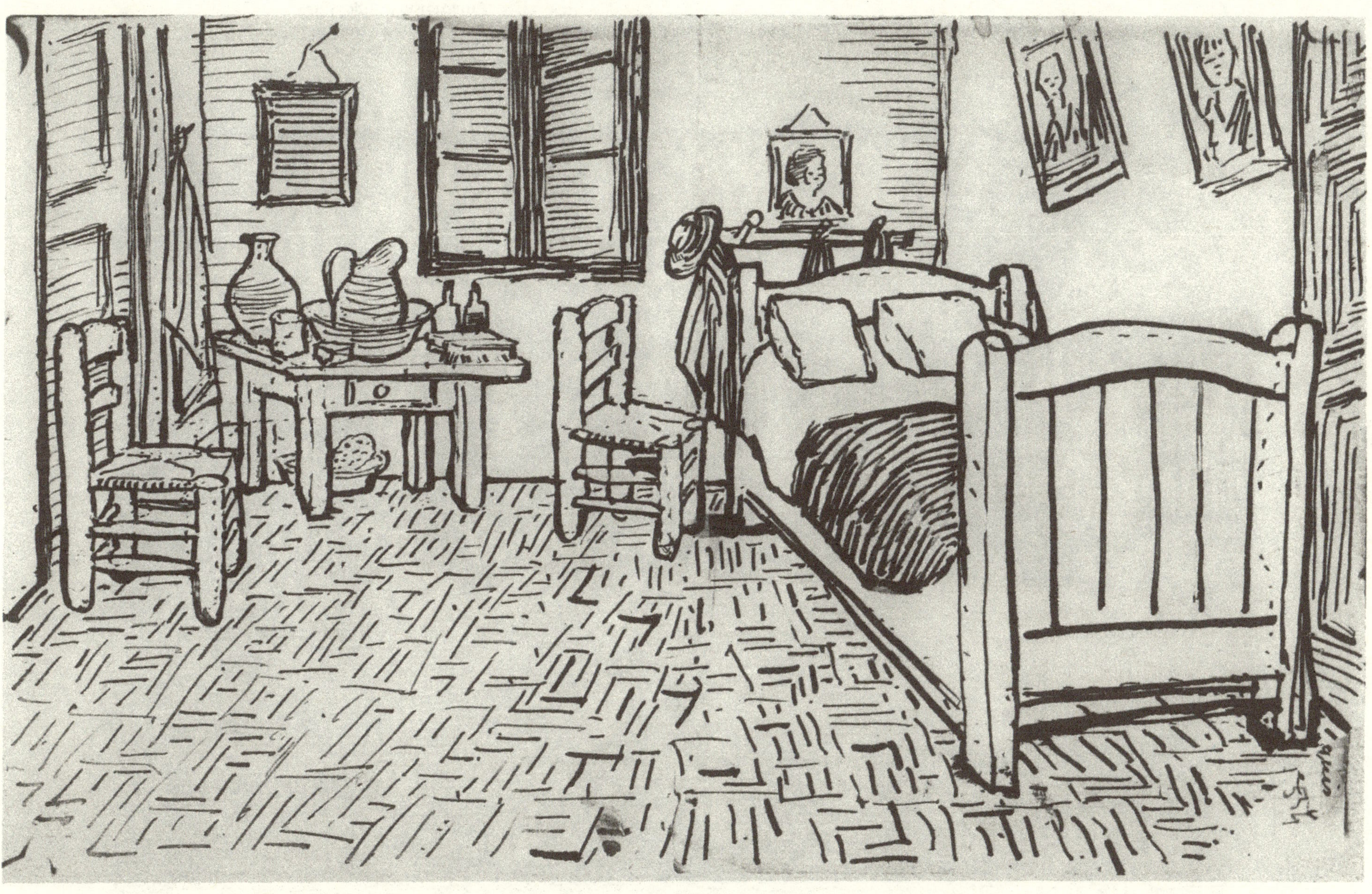

Vincent's bedroom. 1888. Pen-and-ink sketch in a letter. (Van Gogh Foundation/National Museum Vincent van Gogh, Amsterdam.)

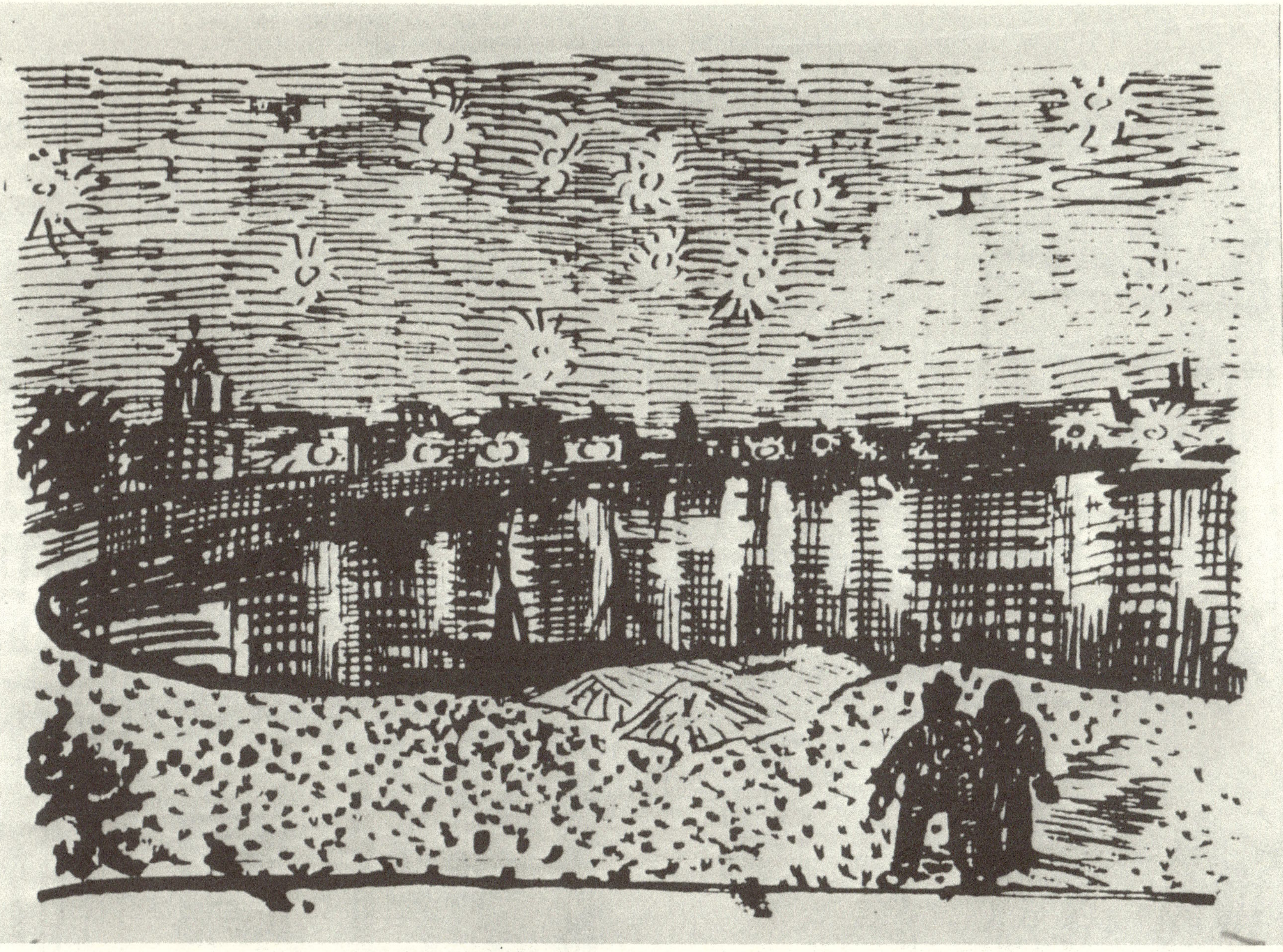

The starry night. 1888. Pen-and-ink sketch in a letter. (Van Gogh Foundation/National Museum Vincent van Gogh, Amsterdam.)

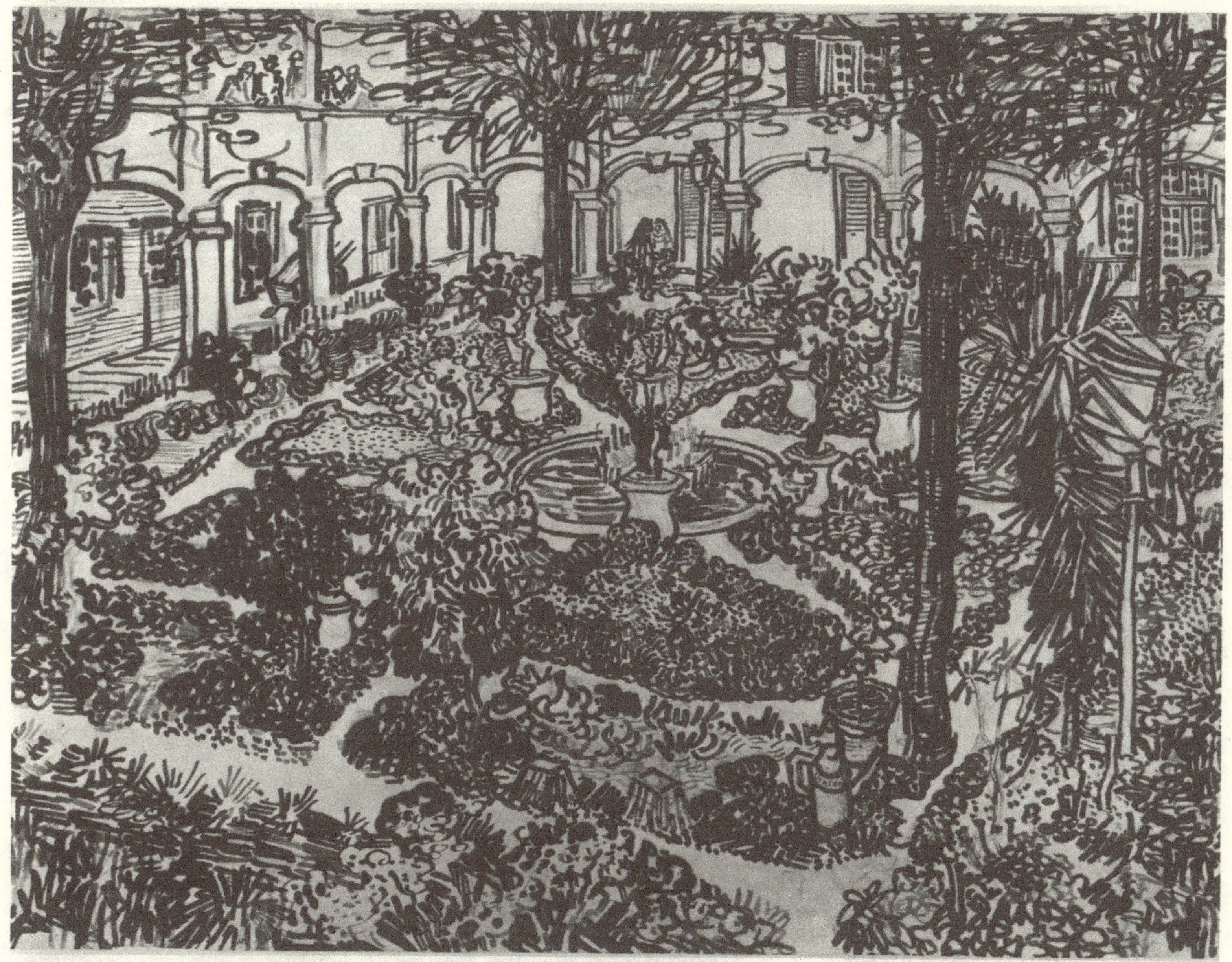

Courtyard of the hospital in Arles. 1889. Pencil, reed pen and brown ink; 45.5 × 59 cm. (Van Gogh Foundation/National Museum Vincent van Gogh, Amsterdam.)

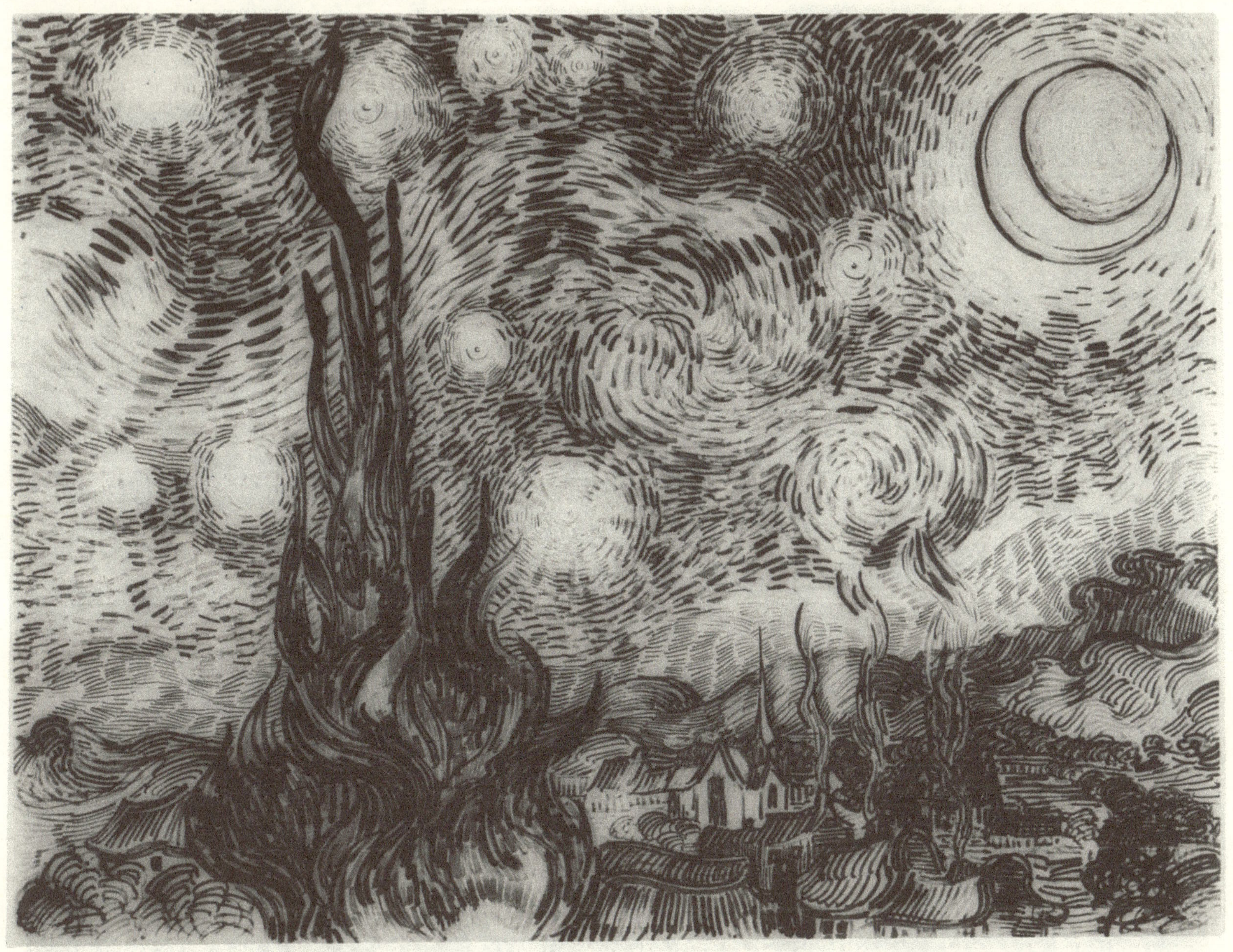

The starry night. 1889. Pen and ink; 47 × 62.5 cm. (destroyed). (Photograph: Netherlands Institute for Art History, The Hague.)

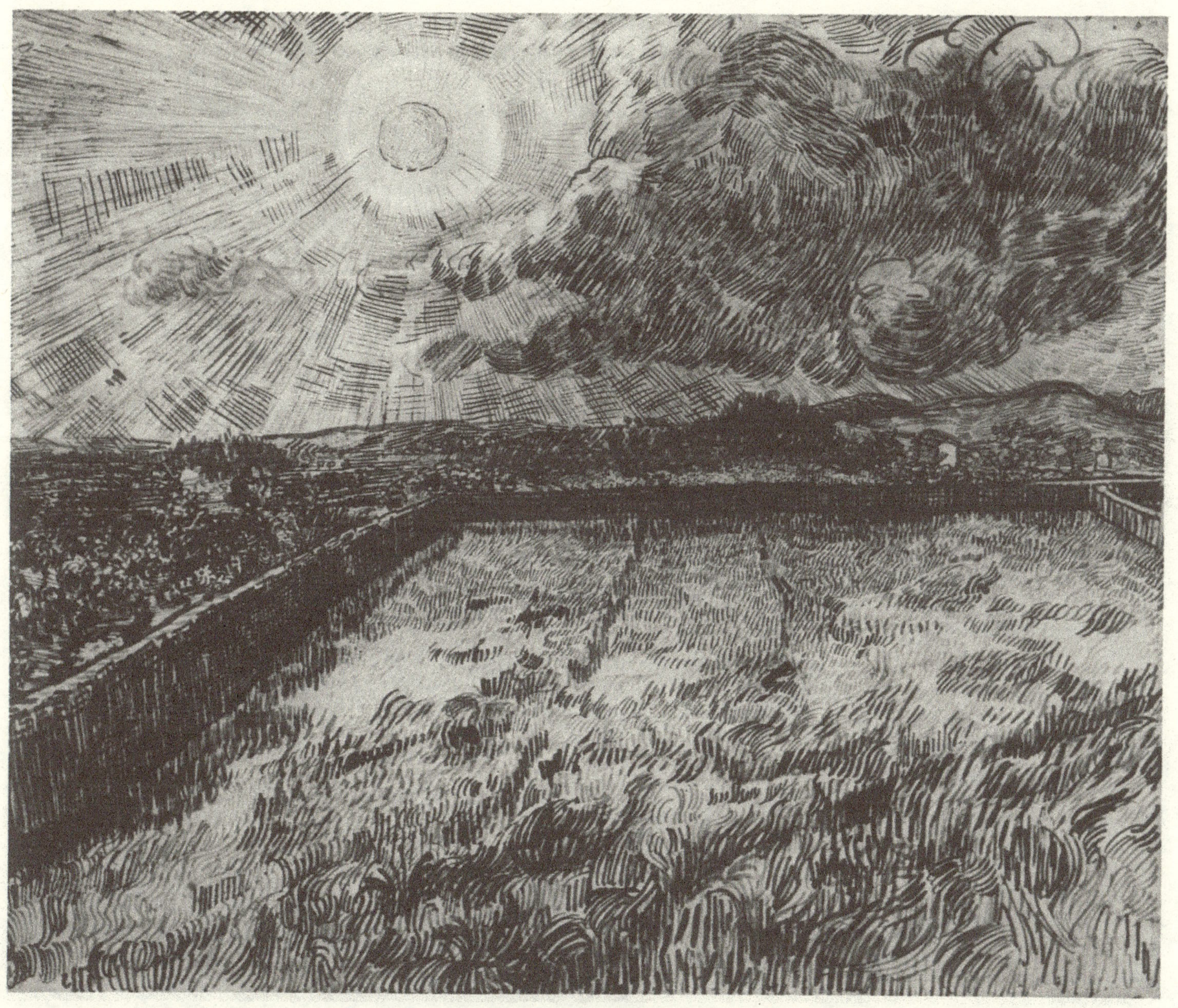

Sun over walled wheat field. 1889. Black chalk, pen and brown ink, heightened with white; 47.5 × 56 cm.
(State Museum Kröller-Müller, Otterlo, The Netherlands.)

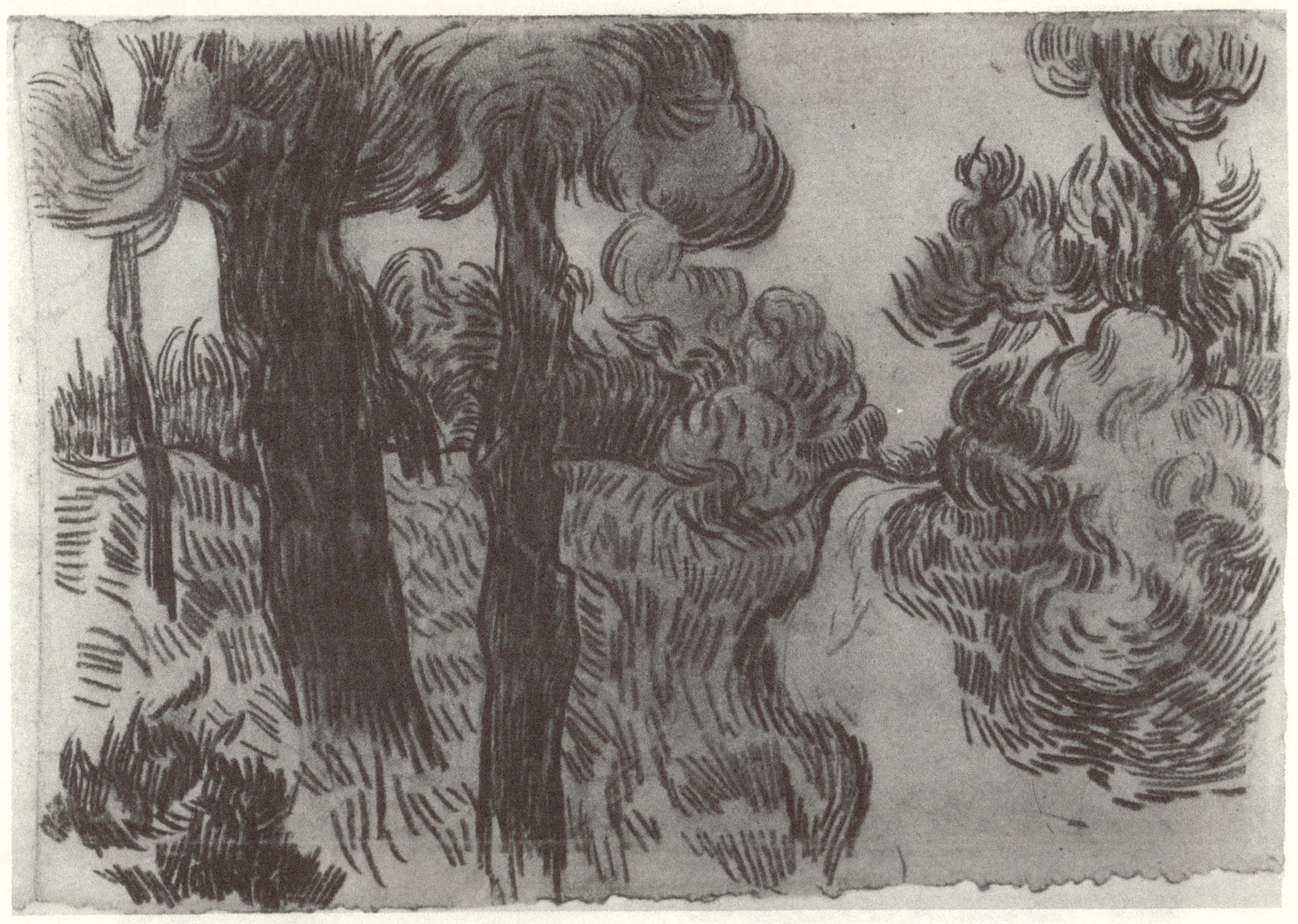

Path between pine trees. 1889. Black chalk; 20.5 × 30 cm. (Van Gogh Foundation/National Museum Vincent van Gogh, Amsterdam.)

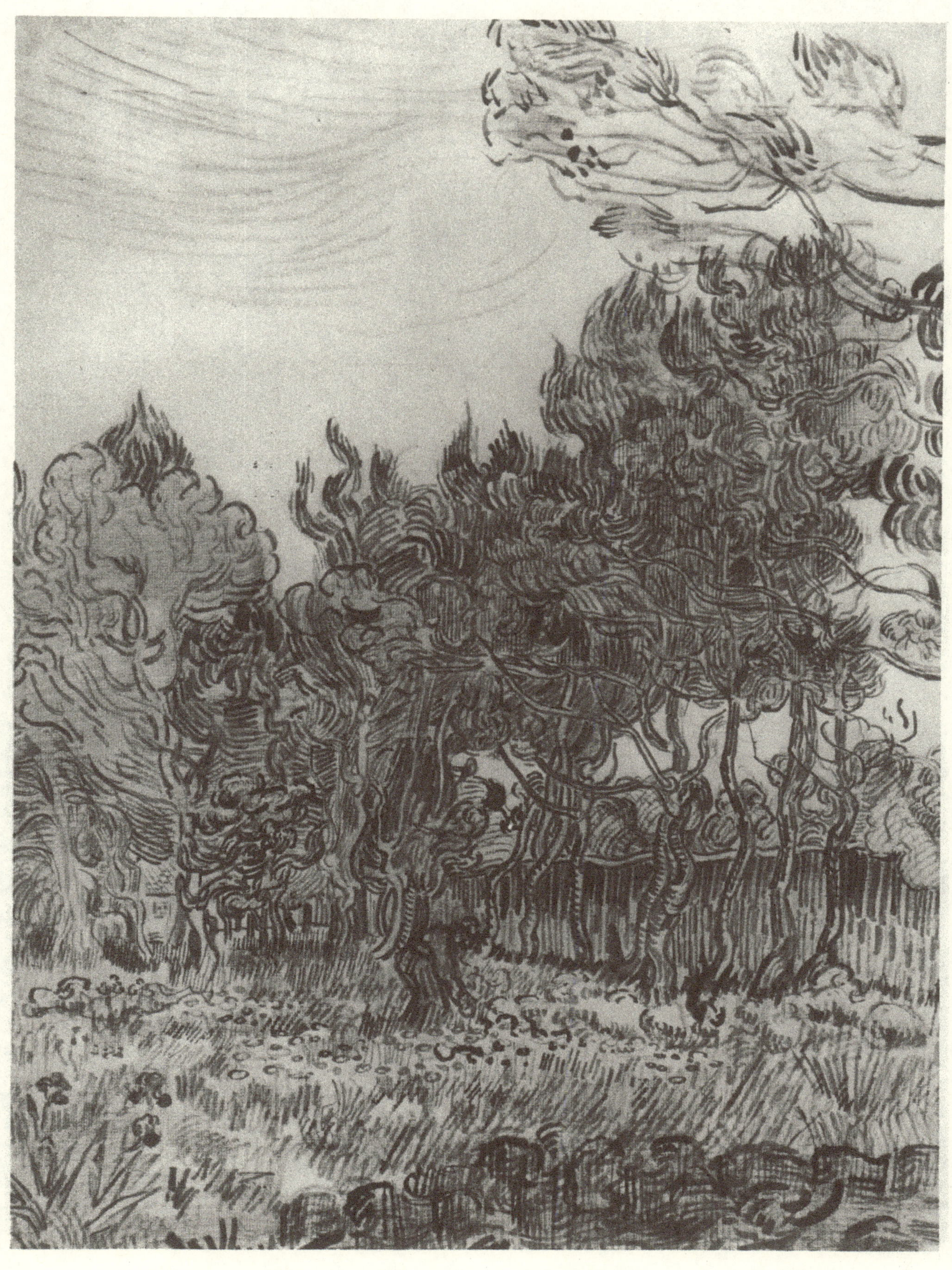

Pine trees near the wall of the asylum at Saint-Rémy. 1889. Reed pen and ink; 63.5 × 48 cm. (The Tate Gallery, London.)

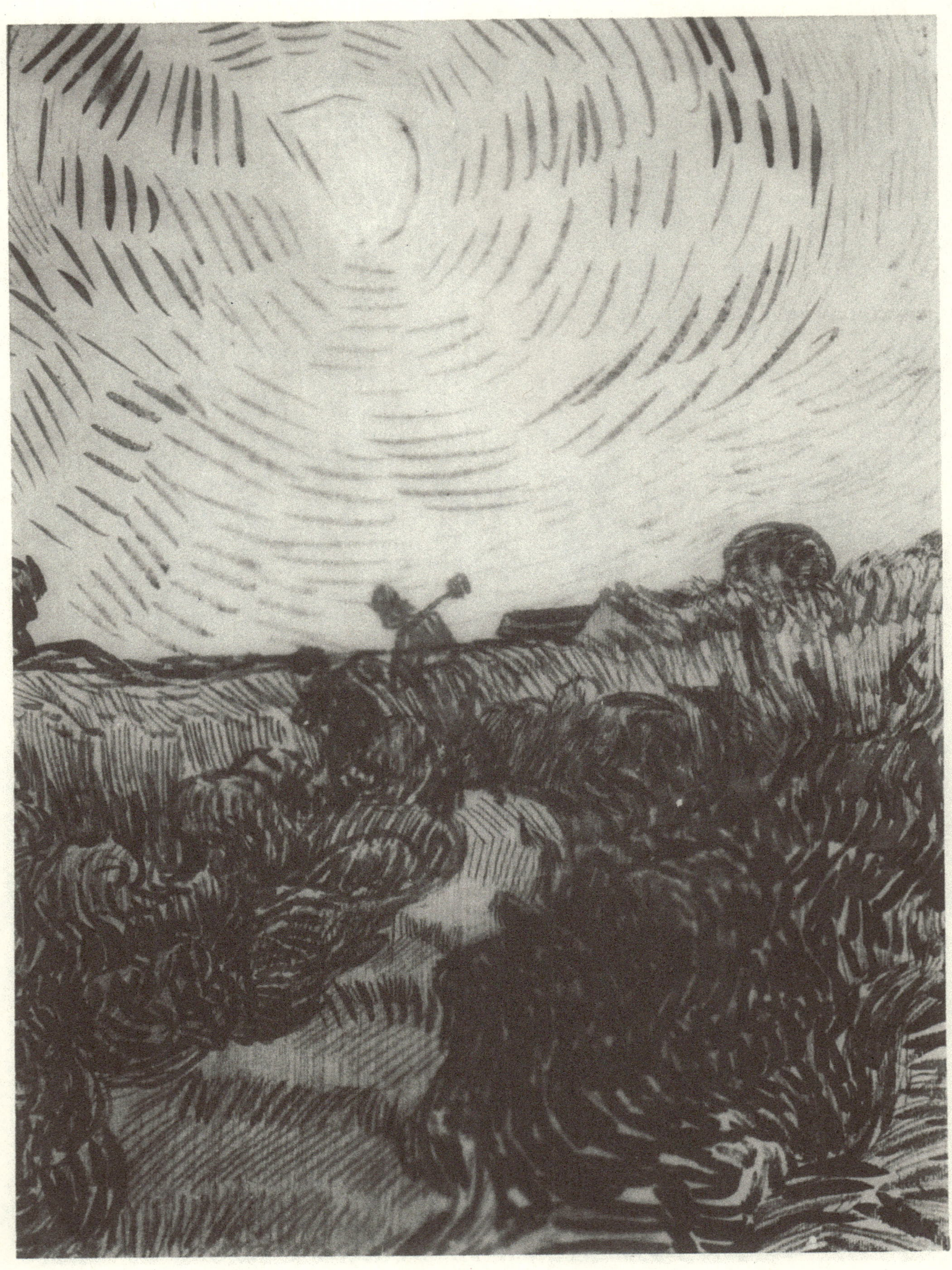

Sun disk above a path between shrubs. 1890. Pen, reed pen, brush and ink; 63 × 48 cm. (Photograph: Netherlands Institute for Art History, The Hague.)

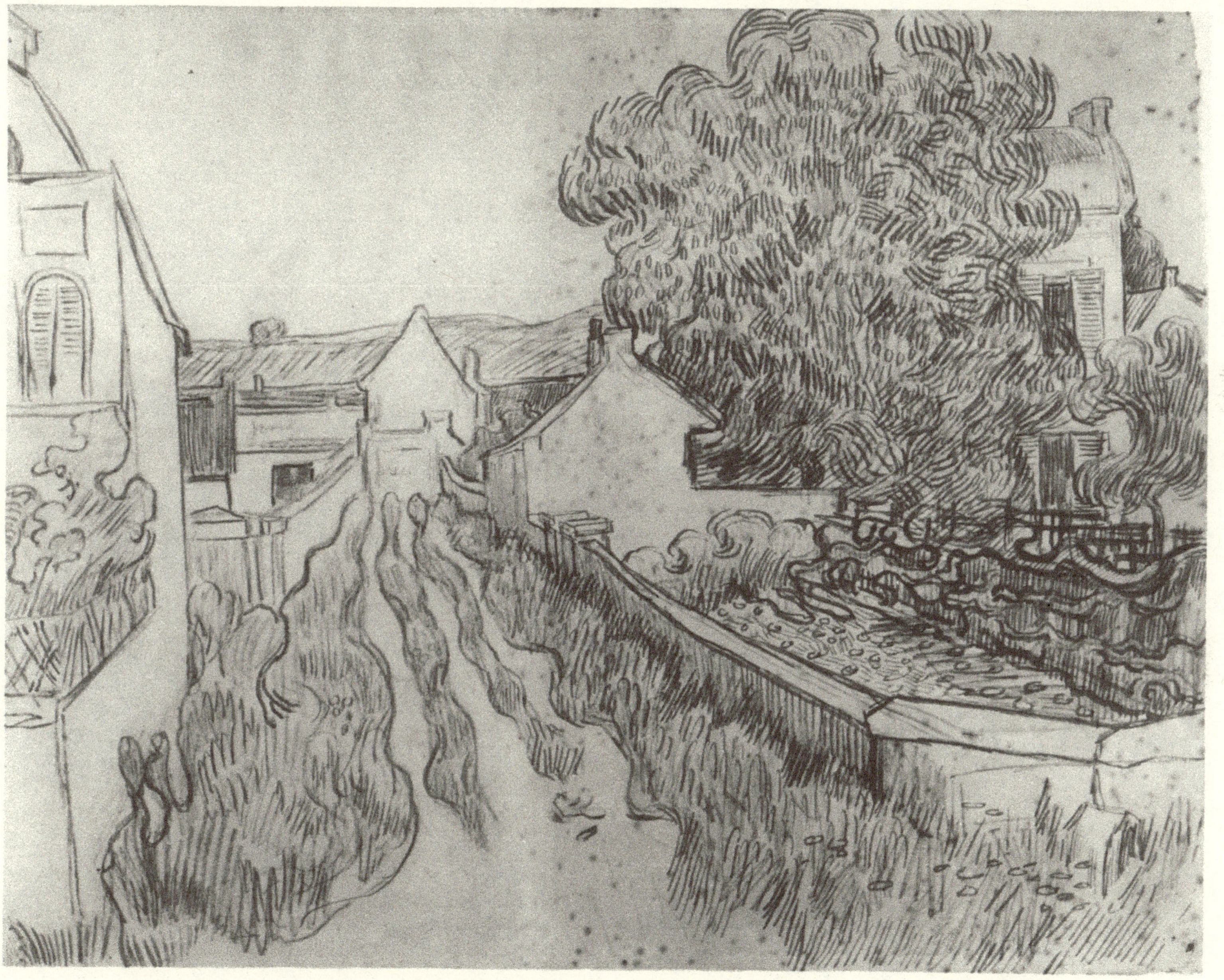

Village street. 1890. Pencil, pen and brown ink; 44.5 × 55 cm. (Van Gogh Foundation/National Museum Vincent van Gogh, Amsterdam.)

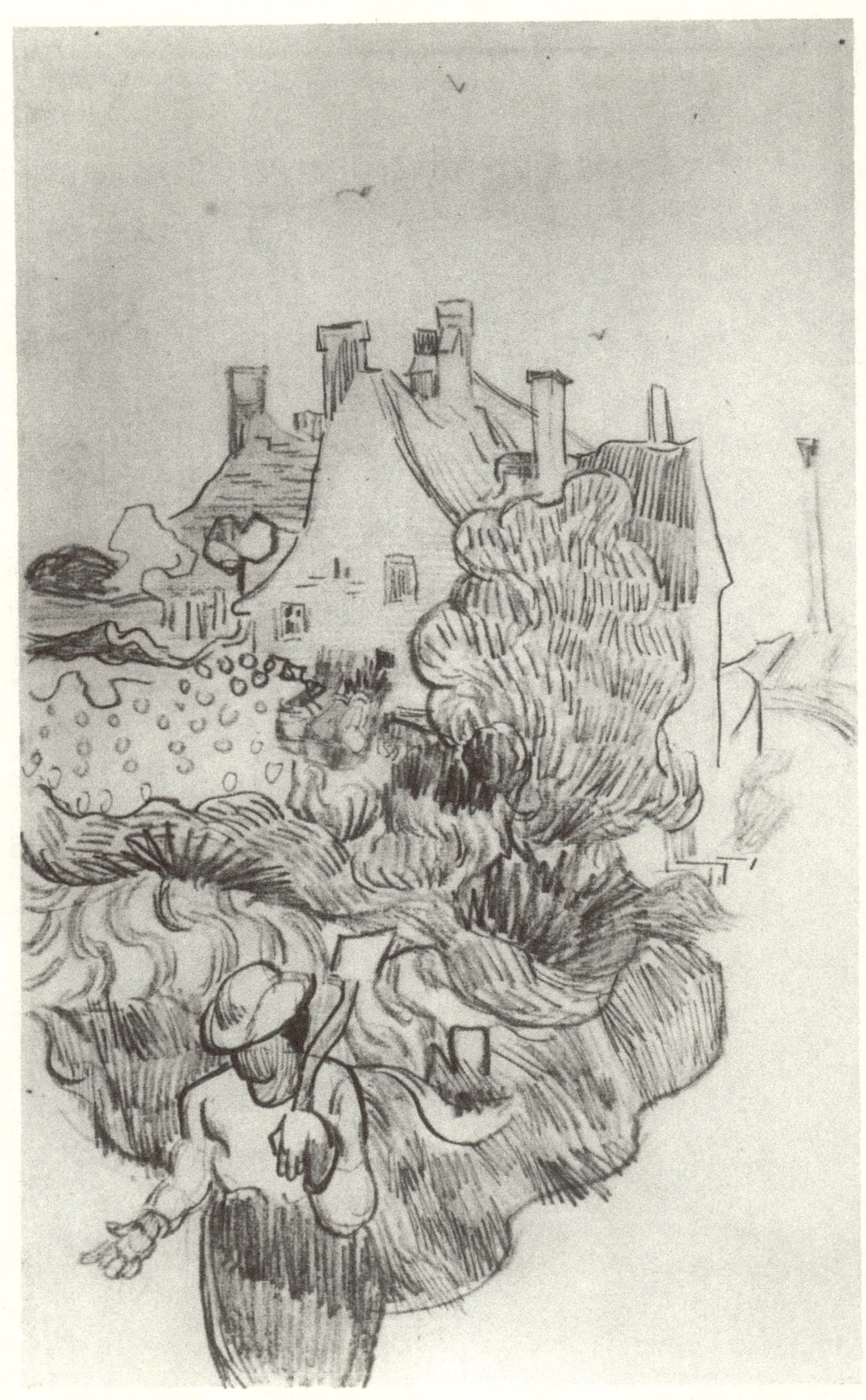

Woman with a spade on a road with houses in the background. 1890. Pencil and black chalk; 44.5 × 27.5 cm. (Van Gogh Foundation/National Museum Vincent van Gogh, Amsterdam.)

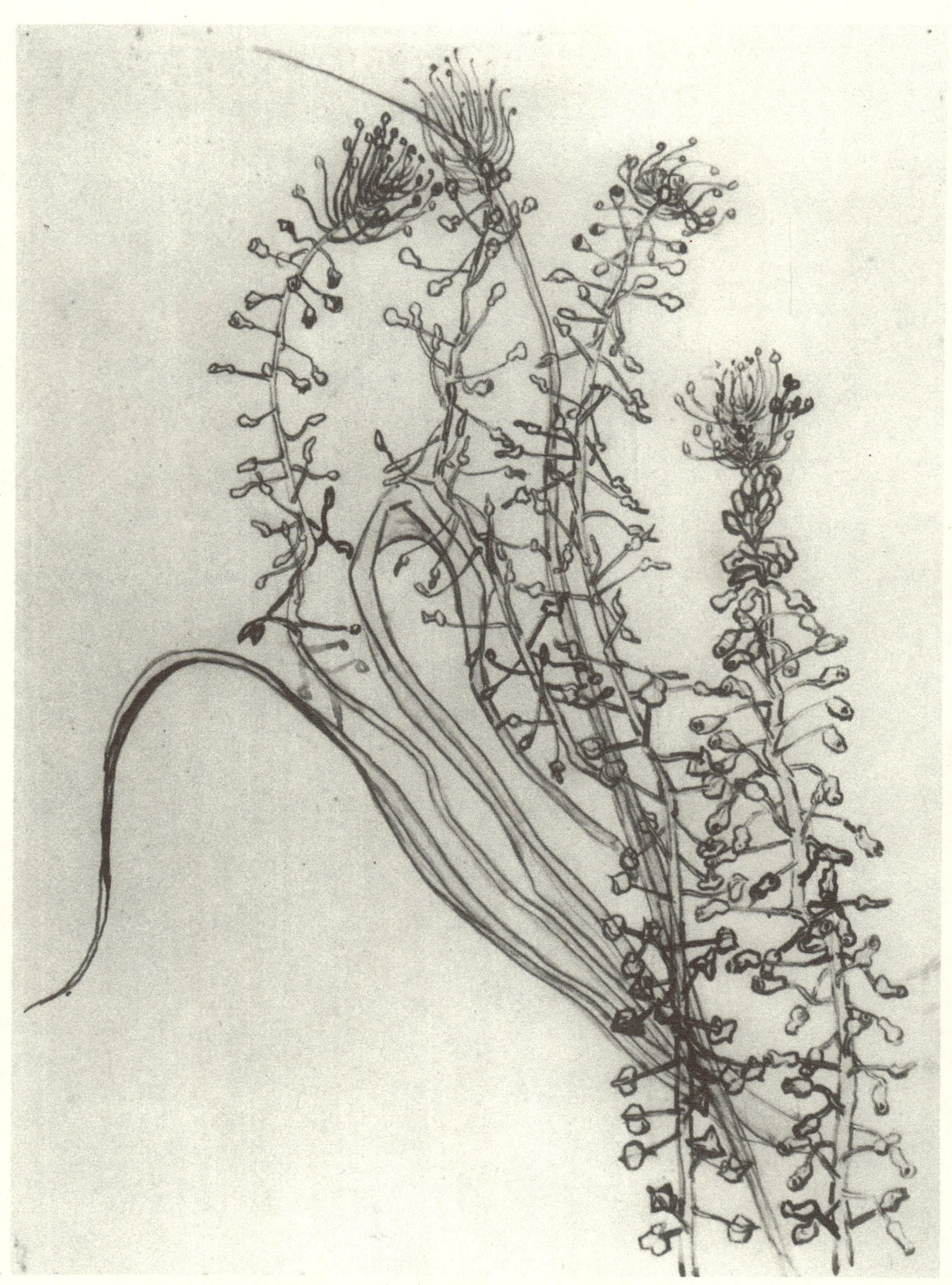

Blossoming branches. 1890. Pencil, reed pen and brown ink; 41 × 31 cm. (Van Gogh Foundation/National Museum Vincent van Gogh, Amsterdam.)